Jud

inspiration

Student's Book 2

MACMILLAN

1 MAKING FRIENDS

This is YTV

Present simple: *be*
Introducing yourself and others
Talking about nationality

1 Presentation

🎧 Read and listen.

I'm Paula and this is YTV from London. We're in Trafalgar Square and these are the winners of our holiday competition! Their prize is a holiday in London!

Hi! I'm Carol and I'm English. I'm from York.

Hi! I'm from Barcelona.

I'm Pedro and I'm from Rio de Janeiro in Brazil. And this is Laura – she's from Spain.

YTV HOLIDAY COMPETITION
WIN A WEEK IN LONDON!

Call us with your answer today.

1 London is
   A 1,000 years old   B 2,000 years old   C 3,000 years old
2 The population of Greater London is
   A 12,500,000   B 10,000,000   C 7,500,000
3 London's river is called
   A Trafalgar   B Big Ben   C the Thames

🇬🇧 0800 444 796   🇨🇭 900 999 999   🇵🇱 800 654 8721

Hi! I'm Ben. I'm from New York.

I'm Jack and I'm English, from Newcastle. This is Tomasz, and he's from Warsaw in Poland.

I'm Sally. I'm from Melbourne in Australia.

My friends call me Tomek for short!

Hello. My name is Gabi and I'm from Zurich in Switzerland.

2 Comprehension

Answer the questions.

1 Where is Jack from?
2 What is the name of the Spanish girl?
3 Who is from Warsaw?
4 What is the name of the American boy?
5 What is the name of the English girl?
6 Where is Pedro from?
7 What is the name of the Swiss girl?
8 Who is from Australia?
9 Who is the YTV presenter?

3 Speaking

Ask and answer questions about the people in the photo.

What's his/her name?

Where's he/she from?

➡ Grammar Summary page 109

7

1 MAKING FRIENDS

1 Do you really speak Chinese?
Present simple
Talking about states and routines

1 Opener

Who is in the photo? Where are they?

2 Presentation

Read and listen.

SALLY Oh, look at those birds! I love them!
CAROL Do you? I don't like pigeons at all.
JACK So what things do you like? How about computers?
CAROL No, I never play on computers.
JACK I don't play on my computer, I chat to people online. That's different. What about films?
CAROL I don't often go to the cinema.
SALLY I do. I go to the movies on Saturdays – after aerobics.
CAROL Oh, I do aerobics too – every Tuesday. My mum teaches aerobics.
JACK And what languages do you speak?
CAROL Oh, let's see – Italian, French and Chinese!
JACK Chinese? Do you really speak Chinese?
CAROL Of course not. It's a joke, silly!
JACK Oh. I know a good joke! What do sea monsters eat?
SALLY I don't know. What do they eat?
JACK Fish and ships!

3 Comprehension

True or false? Correct the false sentences.

1 Carol loves pigeons.
2 Jack doesn't like computers.
3 Sally goes to the cinema every Tuesday.
4 Sally and Carol do aerobics every week.
5 Carol's mother teaches aerobics.
6 Carol speaks Chinese.
7 Jack knows a joke about sea monsters.

4 Grammar

Complete.

> **Present simple**
> I _____ to the movies on Saturdays.
> She **loves** pigeons.
> Carol _____ Italian.
> What languages _____ you speak?
> Do you really _____ Chinese?
> I _____n't play on my computer.
> She _____n't speak Chinese.
>
> We use the present simple to describe states, routines and regular actions.

➡ Check the answers: Grammar Summary page 109

5 Grammar Practice

Complete the sentences with the correct form of the verb.

1 Sally _____ pigeons. (love)
2 She _____ to the cinema on Saturdays. (go)
3 Carol _____ computers. (not like)
4 Jack _____ to people online. (chat)
5 He _____ on his computer. (not play)
6 Carol and Sally _____ aerobics. (do)
7 _____ they _____ lots of films? (see)
8 _____ Carol _____ Chinese? (speak)
9 What _____ sea monsters _____ ? (eat)
10 _____ you _____ the answer? (know)

6 Listening

🎧 Listen and complete the sentences.

WINNERS' WORLD YTV

_____ goes swimming every Friday evening.
_____ speaks four languages.
_____ loves hip-hop and rap.
_____ likes computers and loves fish and chips.

7 Pronunciation

🎧 Listen and repeat.

/s/ chats	/z/ does	/ɪz/ watches
drinks	knows	chooses
eats	loves	finishes

Now listen and write these words in the correct column.

goes   likes   plays   relaxes   speaks   teaches

8 Game

Practise spelling.

How do you spell 'aerobics'?

A-E-R-O-B-I-C-S.

Correct! One point!

9 Speaking

Ask other students and complete the chart. You can write the questions first!

Do you play football every week?

Yes, I do.

No, I don't.

Find someone who …	Name
doesn't play football every week.	
drinks tea at breakfast.	
doesn't do aerobics.	
speaks three languages.	
often watches TV.	
doesn't go to bed late.	
often phones friends.	
doesn't chat online.	

10 Writing

Look at the activities in exercise 9, and write sentences about what other students do and don't do.

Marek doesn't play football every week.
Joanna drinks tea at breakfast.

Now write five sentences about yourself.

I play football every week. I don't drink tea at breakfast, I drink coffee …

1 MAKING FRIENDS

2 You're standing on my foot!

Present continuous
Describing what's happening now

1 Opener

Look at the photo and find these as quickly as possible.

a badge   a bag   a busker   a camera   a fleece
flowers   a guitar   a hat   a map   an umbrella

2 Presentation

Read and listen.

The YTV group are sightseeing in Covent Garden.
BEN   What's happening? I can't see a thing.
CAROL Greg is telling everyone about Covent Garden.
BEN   Who's Greg?
CAROL He's the tour guide. He's standing next to Laura. He's wearing a YTV badge.
BEN   What are Pedro and Gabi doing? Oh, look, they're holding hands!
CAROL No, they aren't holding hands! She's helping him with his camera.
BEN   Let me see!
CAROL Ow! You're standing on my foot!
BEN   Sorry. Hey, what's that man doing?
CAROL Who do you mean? The busker?
BEN   No, I'm talking about the tall man. He's standing behind the girl in the red hat. Look!
CAROL Is he helping her?
BEN   No, he isn't helping her. He's putting his hand in her bag. I think he's taking her purse.
CAROL Quick, let's stop him!
BEN   He's running this way!

3 Comprehension

Match the questions with the answers. There is one wrong answer.

1 Who is standing next to Laura?
2 Is Tomek wearing a YTV badge?
3 Are Pedro and Gabi holding hands?
4 Is Gabi taking photographs?
5 Is Gabi helping Pedro?
6 What is Ben doing when Carol says 'Ow!'?
7 Where is the tall man standing?
8 What is the tall man doing?

a Behind the girl in the red hat.
b No, she isn't.
c Yes, they are.
d He's putting his hand in her bag.
e Greg.
f No, they aren't.
g No, he isn't.
h He's standing on her foot.
i Yes, she is.

4 Grammar

Complete.

Present continuous
You're stand**ing** on my foot.
He's _____ a YTV badge.
They're hold**ing** hands.
What _____ they do**ing**?
_____ he help**ing** her?
He _____n't help**ing** her.
They _____n't hold**ing** hands.

We use the present continuous to talk about temporary events and what is happening now.

➡ Check the answers: Grammar Summary page 109

5 Grammar Practice

Write sentences using the present continuous.

Ben/wear/an orange fleece
Ben is wearing an orange fleece.

1 Greg/talk/about Covent Garden
2 Tomek/visit/London for the first time
3 Tomek and Laura/look/at the map?
4 Pedro and Gabi/not hold/hands!
5 the tall man/steal/the girl's purse?
6 the busker/play/the guitar
7 Jack and Sally/watch/the busker
8 Ben/not listen/to Greg

6 Listening

Who is the tall man? Why is he running? What happens next?

Now listen and see if you are right.

7 Pronunciation

Listen and count the syllables. Mark the stress.

busker   camera   garden   guitar   happening
orange   sightseeing   video

■ *busker* 2

Now listen again and repeat.

8 Speaking

Look at the photo of the YTV group in Covent Garden. Ask and answer questions about what people are wearing.

What's Gabi wearing?
She's wearing black trousers and a pink top.
Who's wearing …?

Clothes
fleece   hat   jacket   jeans   pullover   shirt   shoes
sweatshirt   top   trainers   trousers   T-shirt

Now ask and answer questions about what people are doing.

What's the girl in the red hat doing?
She's watching the busker.

9 Writing

Write sentences describing the people in the photo. Don't write their names!

He is standing on the right. He is wearing a blue pullover. He is holding an umbrella in his left hand.

Now give your sentences to another student. Can he/she guess the names?

1 MAKING FRIENDS

3 What's the producer's job?

Possessive adjectives and pronouns
Possessive *'s* and *s'*
Present simple and present continuous
Expressing possession

1 Opener

Which of these can you see in the photo?

bangles   a briefcase   a busker   a dog   glasses   trees
lights   a magazine   a pigeon   a scarf   sunglasses

2 Presentation

Read and listen.

GREG   OK, everyone – come and meet my boss, Kate Dixon. She's a YTV producer.

KATE   Hi! I hope you're having a great time here in London! Now it's the actors' coffee break, so I can tell you what we're doing. We're making a film for YTV about tourists in London. Today we're looking at a problem for some tourists – pickpockets.

TOMEK   Excuse me, what are 'pickpockets'?

KATE   Pickpockets steal things from people's pockets and their bags. They're a problem in lots of cities.

CAROL   What do *you* do? I mean, what's the producer's job?

KATE   The producer is in charge of the film. I make sure that the film is good, and that it isn't too expensive! Hey, Greg, you're drinking my coffee!

GREG   Are you sure it's yours?

KATE   I know it's mine.

GREG   You're right! It's got sugar in it. Ugh!

3 Comprehension

Give short answers to the questions.

1 Who is Greg's boss?
2 What is Kate's job?
3 What is Kate's film about?
4 What do pickpockets do?
5 Whose coffee is Greg drinking?
6 Whose coffee hasn't got sugar in it?

4 Speaking

Look carefully at the photo. Ask and answer questions about these things.

red bag   glasses   map   purple scarf   bangles
notebook   YTV badge   briefcase   grey skirt

Whose is the red bag?
It's Carol's.

Whose are the glasses?
They're …

12

5 Grammar

Complete.

Possessive adjectives		Possessive pronouns	
my	our	_____	ours
your	your	_____	yours
his/her	_____	his/hers	theirs

Possessive 's and s'
Singular noun — the producer**'s** job
Plural noun — the actor**s'** coffee break
Irregular plural noun — people**'s** pockets

➡ Check the answers: Grammar Summary page 110

6 Grammar Practice

Complete with possessive pronouns.

It isn't his coffee. It's her coffee.
The coffee isn't _his_. It's _hers_.

1 This isn't your map. It's my map.
   The map isn't _____. It's _____.
2 These aren't our coffees. They're their coffees.
   These coffees aren't _____. They're _____.
3 It isn't her camera. It's his camera.
   The camera isn't _____. It's _____.
4 They aren't your sandwiches. They're our sandwiches.
   The sandwiches aren't _____. They're _____.

7 Speaking

Look at the photo. Ask and answer.

Greg's coffee?

> Is it Greg's coffee?
> No, it isn't his. It's Kate's.

1 Carol's watch?   4 Tomek's briefcase?
2 Kate's notebook?   5 Greg's glasses?
3 Laura's bangles?   6 Jack's magazine?

8 Listening

🎧 Listen and match the words for jobs with their definitions.

1 The producer …
2 The scriptwriter …
3 The cameraman …
4 The director …
5 The actors …
6 The stuntmen and women …

a has the camera and shoots the film.
b play the different parts.
c tells the actors what to do.
d is in charge of the film.
e do dangerous things, like fights and car crashes.
f writes the film.

9 Pronunciation

🎧 Listen and repeat.

> break   case   eat   great   make
> mean   meet   play   speak   steal

Now write the words under /iː/ or /eɪ/ in the chart. Then listen again and check.

/iː/	/eɪ/
eat	break

10 Speaking

Ask and answer questions about these people in the photo. Use the present simple and present continuous.

> the producer   the cameraman
> the director   the actors

> What does the producer do?
> The producer makes sure …

> What is the producer doing?
> She's talking …

11 Writing

The cameraman is talking to Paula on his mobile phone. He is describing what is happening. What do you think he is saying? Write at least five sentences.

We're making a film in Covent Garden about pickpockets. The actors are having their coffee break and …

UNIT 1

13

1 MAKING FRIENDS

4 Integrated Skills
Personal profiles

FIVE MINUTES WITH ... GABI

Gabi is one of the winners of our London holiday competition. What's she like? Find out here!

Where do you live?
In Zurich in Switzerland, but at the moment I'm staying at the Royal Hotel in London.

What are your favourite clothes?
It depends. I often wear jeans and a sweatshirt, but I like short skirts in the summer.

What is your favourite English word?
(1) _____

And your favourite colours?
(2) _____

What makes you angry?
People who don't listen.

What makes you happy?
Sunshine and blue sky!

How do you relax?
(3) _____

What languages do you speak?
(4) _____

Is there someone very important to you?
What do you mean? Have I got a boyfriend? I'm not telling you! But my mother is very important to me.

Is there something special you do every day?
(5) _____

What are you reading at the moment?
An English book called *L.A. Winners*. It's great!

UNIT 1

1 Opener

Guess: What languages does Gabi speak? What are her favourite colours?

Reading

2 Read *Five Minutes with … Gabi* and complete the answers with sentences a–e.

a I listen to music.
b German, of course, and French. And I'm learning English.
c That's easy. Pink, pink, pink. And then black!
d 'Sorry'. The English say 'sorry' all the time!
e That's difficult. Let me think. I know. I try to help someone every day.

Now listen and check.

3 Here are Tomek's answers to some of the same questions. Which questions?

1 Good music.
2 People who don't tell the truth.
3 I play the guitar.
4 My girlfriend. I'm looking forward to seeing her again.
5 I cycle five kilometres before breakfast every morning.

4 Listening

Read this profile. Then listen to an interview with Ben and correct the six mistakes in the profile.

BEN SERRANO

Ben is our winner from the USA and he's from California. He's 17 and lives at home with his parents and sister, Rose. His favourite clothes are shorts and his baseball cap.

Ben's favourite colours are red, white and green and his favourite word is Yes!. Nothing makes him angry and his friends make him happy.

Ben relaxes by playing with his dog DJ in the park. He speaks English, of course, and he's learning French. His friends are very important to him and he's missing them now he's in London. Finally, Ben watches TV for half an hour every evening.

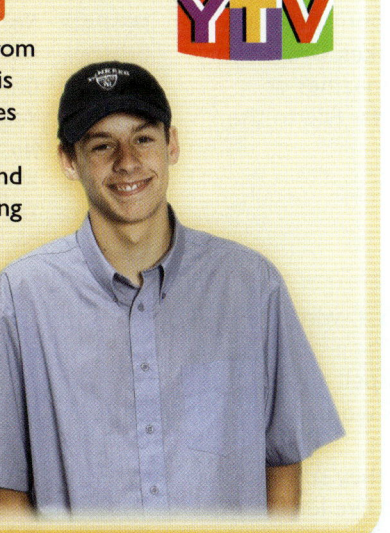

5 Speaking

Ask another student the questions in *Five Minutes with … Gabi*. Note down the answers.

6 Writing

Look at the profile of Ben. Match the information in each paragraph with the questions in *Five Minutes with … Gabi*.

Now write a three-paragraph profile of the student you interviewed in exercise 5.

Learner Independence

7 Different people learn in different ways. What is your favourite way of finding the meaning of a word? Order these ways 1–5 (1 = best, 5 = worst).

- Use a bilingual dictionary.
- Use an English–English dictionary.
- Ask your teacher for help.
- Guess from the text.
- Ask another student.

Now compare with another student.

8 Make your own personal phrasebook. Choose English expressions from this unit that you want to learn and write the translation next to each expression.

9 Phrasebook

Listen and repeat these useful expressions.

Then find them in this unit.

> That's different.
> Of course not.
> It's a joke, silly!
> Ow!
> Let me see!
> Hey!
> Excuse me.
> What do you do?
> You're right!
> It depends.
> What do you mean?

Now write a four-line dialogue using one or more of the expressions.

A *What do you do?*
B *I'm a secret agent.*
A *Really?*
B *Of course not. It's a joke, silly!*

Unit 1 Communication Activity
Student A page 106
Student B page 116

1 MAKING FRIENDS
Inspiration *Extra!*

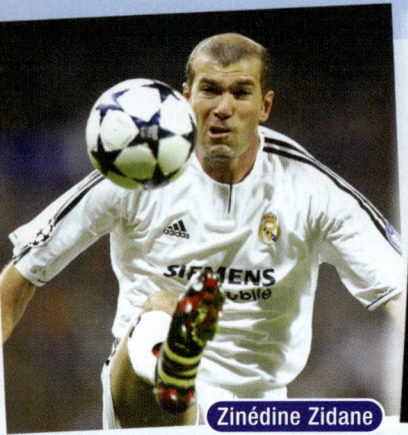

Zinédine Zidane

Ms Dynamite

Jude Law

Norah Jones

PROJECT Star File

Make a file about your favourite stars.

1 Work in a group and look again at pages 14–15. Then make a list of your favourite stars. Choose two or three to write about.

2 Find out information about the stars, for example:

> Birthday   Favourite TV programme
> Favourite film   Favourite music
> Favourite food/drink   Favourite clothes
> Favourite colours   Favourite day   Mistakes
> Something special   Their website

3 Work together and make a Star File about the stars. Read it carefully and correct any mistakes. Draw pictures or find photographs from magazines or newspapers for your file. Show your Star File to the other groups.

GAME Spelling Chain

- Form two teams.
- Student 1 from Team A says and spells a word of five or more letters.
- Student 1 from Team B must say and spell a word that begins with the last letter of Team A's word.
- Student 2 from Team A continues …
- Teams score one point for each word they spell correctly. All words must have at least five letters. If a team cannot continue, they lose a point.

A Pocket P-O-C-K-E-T
B Trousers T-R-O-U-S-E-R-S
A Sugar S-U-G-A-R
B Relax R-E-L-A-X
A ?!?!?!

SKETCH *The Ticket Inspector*

🎧 Read and listen.

A passenger is sitting on a train. He is reading a newspaper.

WAITER   Coffee?
PASSENGER No, thanks.

The passenger continues reading. The waiter comes back.

WAITER   Seats for dinner?
PASSENGER No, thanks.

The passenger continues reading.
The ticket inspector speaks to him.

INSPECTOR Tickets!
PASSENGER No, thanks.
INSPECTOR Pardon?
PASSENGER I don't want a ticket, thank you.
INSPECTOR I'm not selling tickets, sir!
PASSENGER No?
INSPECTOR No. I want to see your ticket.
PASSENGER Oh, I haven't got one.
INSPECTOR You haven't got a ticket?
PASSENGER No, I never buy a ticket.
INSPECTOR Why not?
PASSENGER They're very expensive.
INSPECTOR Sir, you're travelling on a train. When you travel by train, you buy a ticket.
PASSENGER I don't.
INSPECTOR I see. All right. Then please leave the train.
PASSENGER What?
INSPECTOR Leave the train.
PASSENGER I can't leave the train!
INSPECTOR Why not?
PASSENGER It's moving!
INSPECTOR Not now, sir. At the next station.
PASSENGER Oh.
INSPECTOR And we're coming to a station now. Here we are, sir. Please leave the train.
PASSENGER Now?
INSPECTOR Yes, sir. Sorry.
PASSENGER Oh, that's OK.
INSPECTOR What?
PASSENGER That's OK.
INSPECTOR OK?
PASSENGER Yes, this is my station. Goodbye!

Adapted from a sketch by Doug Case

Now act out the sketch in pairs or groups of three.

UNIT 1

REVISION for more practice

THIS IS YTV

Look at the characters in the photo on pages 6–7. Write six questions and answers.

Where's Tomek from?
He's from Poland.

LESSON 1

Look at the conversation on page 8. Write two sentences each about Jack, Sally and Carol using the present simple.

Sally loves pigeons. She goes to the cinema …

LESSON 2

Look at the photo on page 10. Write questions and answers about what people are doing/wearing.

What's Laura doing?
She's looking at the map.

LESSON 3

Make a list of clothes and other things that people wear. Use the photo on page 12 to give you ideas.

jacket, sunglasses, …

LESSON 4

Look at the YTV profile of Ben on page 15. Write a similar profile of Gabi using information from the article on page 14.

Gabi is our winner from Switzerland and she lives in Zurich. Her favourite clothes …

EXTENSION for language development

THIS IS YTV

Look at this conversation. Write similar conversations about famous people.

A His name is Michael Johnson.
B Is he Australian?
A No, he isn't. He's American.

LESSON 1

Choose two friends or members of your family. Write sentences about:

- what they love
- what they do at weekends
- what they never do
- what languages they speak

My mother loves rock music.

LESSON 2

Look at the photo in Lesson 1 on page 8 and write sentences about Jack, Sally and Carol using the present continuous. What are they doing/wearing and where are they standing?

Sally is pointing at the pigeons.
She's wearing …

LESSON 3

Look at the photo on page 12. Write questions and answers about these things.

| blue jacket | white shoes | mobile phone |
| magazine | coffees | red hat | watch | grey trainers |

Whose is the blue jacket?
It's the director's.

LESSON 4

Look at Ben's profile on page 15. Write a similar profile of yourself – in the third person singular – for the YTV magazine.

17

culture

1 Reading

Read the London sightseeing guide and match the places with the photos.

Welcome to London

A The London Eye
It's new, and it's fun. Ride up in the sky and look down on London. The London Eye is 135 metres high and is the slowest big wheel in the world. It has 32 capsules which carry 25 passengers each. The London Eye is on the South Bank of the Thames in the exact centre of London.

B The Monument
Another good place to see London from the sky. You can climb to the top of the 300-year-old Monument and look out over the city. It's the tallest stone column in the world. The column is exactly 61.5 metres tall and 61.5 metres from where the Great Fire of London started in 1666.

C St Paul's Cathedral
This famous church, rebuilt after the Great Fire, is near the Monument. It's the fifth cathedral on this site. Visit the famous Whispering Gallery – you can hear people whisper 30 metres away!

D Camden Market
London has lots of markets, but Camden is the best. You can buy lots of exciting things here – unusual clothes and some great records. The market is open at the weekend – the best day to go is Sunday. It's London's second most visited tourist attraction (after the British Museum).

E Regent's Canal
You can take a sightseeing boat along the canal from Camden past Regent's Park and London Zoo. There are sightseeing tours every hour from April to October. From November to March the boats only go at the weekend.

F Covent Garden
Once London's biggest flower, fruit and vegetable market, the Covent Garden piazza is now another great place for shopping, and also has lots of cafés and restaurants. You can usually see buskers and street theatre here – but be careful of pickpockets!

G Big Ben
What is Big Ben? Is it a clock? In fact, Big Ben is really the name of one of the clock's bells and it weighs over 13 tonnes. Big Ben is in the clock tower of the Houses of Parliament. The tower is 95.7 metres high and it's on the River Thames.

H Madame Tussaud's
Come here and see models of famous people, from film stars and characters to kings and queens. It's open every day of the year except Christmas Day. A popular attraction is the 'Spirit of London' time ride – you sit in the back of a real black taxi and 'travel' through London's history in five minutes. And don't miss the Chamber of Horrors!

I The London Aquarium
Meet sharks face to face! This aquarium has over 365 kinds of fish – more than one for every day of the year. The aquarium makes its own seawater, and every year it uses salt equal to the weight of nine London double-decker buses. It's on the South Bank of the river, next to the London Eye, and is open every day from 10am–6pm.

culture

2 Comprehension

Find the answers to these questions in the London sightseeing guide.

Where can you …
1. get good views of London?
2. see models of film stars?
3. see sharks?
4. take a boat trip?
5. go shopping?
6. hear a famous bell?

3 Vocabulary

Match the words with their definitions.

1. an attraction
2. an aquarium
3. a busker
4. a cathedral
5. passengers
6. a double-decker
7. a pickpocket

a. someone who plays music in the street for money
b. someone who steals things from people's pockets
c. a place where you can see unusual fish
d. people who are travelling
e. something interesting for people to see or do
f. the most important church in a city
g. a bus with two floors

4 Writing

Write a paragraph for tourists about a famous place in your town/country. Use these questions to help you.

- Where is it?
- What is special about it?
- What can you see/do there?
- When is it open?
- How old is it?

2 FESTIVALS

1 Europe's best street party

Comparative and superlative adjectives
Making comparisons

1 Opener
Why is the woman in the photo wearing a costume?

2 Presentation
Read and listen to *Carnivals*.

3 Comprehension
True or false? Correct the false sentences.
1 In Rio each carnival parade lasts 24 hours.
2 At carnival time hotels in Rio are much more expensive than usual.
3 Carnival in Rio is longer than Notting Hill carnival.
4 Notting Hill carnival is in February or March.
5 The carnival in Notting Hill is less famous than the one in Rio.
6 Notting Hill carnival is the biggest in the world.

CARNIVALS

Carnival in Rio

In Brazil, people celebrate carnival in February or March. Every region has its own festival, but carnival in Rio is the most famous. It lasts four days and millions of people go to it, including 300,000 foreign visitors. It's bigger than any other Brazilian carnival – and better, say the *cariocas* (the people of Rio).

There are two nights of parades in the streets and in the giant samba stadium, which holds 90,000 people. Some parades have thousands of dancers, all in the most amazing costumes, and 600 to 800 drummers. Each parade lasts ten to twelve hours and the judges choose the best dancers. There are also all-night carnival balls with non-stop loud music.

At carnival, Rio is the most exciting city in the world, but it is also one of the most expensive – hotels and taxis cost four times as much as usual. But that's because Rio has the biggest and most spectacular carnival in the world!

Notting Hill carnival

For most of the year, Notting Hill is a smart quiet part of London. But at carnival time you can see the real cosmopolitan Notting Hill, which is much more exciting – and noisier!

The Notting Hill carnival is smaller than Rio and less well-known, but it's the largest carnival in Europe. It started in 1964 and now over a million people come to the carnival for two days at the end of August each year. More than fifty bands parade through the streets in colourful costumes. There are lots of sound systems playing reggae and other kinds of music, and three stages where bands play. The streets are full of people dancing and following the bands. And when you get hungry, there are stalls selling exotic food from all over the world.

They call Notting Hill carnival 'The Greatest Show on Earth'. It's Europe's best street party! And it's less expensive than Rio!

6 Game

Say the comparative and superlative adjectives.

> Good.
>
> Better, best.
>
> Two points!

7 Writing

Read *CARNIVALS* again and complete the chart for Rio and Notting Hill.

	Rio	Notting Hill	Your festival
When?			
How long?			
How many people?			
What kind of music?			
What's special about it?			

Now complete the chart for a festival you know about (in your country or another one).

4 Grammar

Complete.

Adjective	Comparative	Superlative
small	small___	the small**est**
large	large**r**	the ___
big	big___	___ ___
nois**y**	___	the nois**iest**
famous	**more** famous	the ___ famous
exciting	___ exciting	the ___ exciting

Irregular
| good | ___ | the best |
| bad | worse | the worst |

The opposite of *more* is _____ .
The opposite of *most* is *least*.

➡ Check the answers: Grammar Summary page 110

8 Speaking

Look at the chart in exercise 7, and compare the two carnivals and your festival.

> The carnival in Rio lasts longer than the Notting Hill carnival.
>
> The carnival in my country is smaller than Rio, but it is one of the most …

9 Pronunciation

🎧 Listen and repeat. Then circle the /ə/ sound.

/ə/ **better**
carnival   colourful   dancer   famous   longer
parade   region   samba   special   thousand

5 Grammar Practice

Complete with comparative or superlative adjectives.

1 The carnival in Rio is _____ than Notting Hill carnival (large).
2 The Notting Hill carnival is the _____ carnival in Europe. (big)
3 *Cariocas* think that Rio has the _____ carnival in the world. (good)
4 Rio is the _____ carnival in the world. (exciting)
5 It's _____ for Europeans to go to the Notting Hill Carnival. (expensive)
6 Pedro is a _____ dancer than Jack. (good)
7 Jack isn't the _____ dancer in the world! (bad)
8 The carnival parades in Rio last _____ than in Notting Hill. (long)
9 The _____ place in Rio at carnival time is the giant samba stadium. (noisy)
10 People who don't have a lot of money look for the _____ hotel. (expensive)

10 Speaking

Compare three cities in your country. Think about:

age (old)   size (big)   people (nice)
festivals   weather (warm/cold, dry/wet)
shopping   sport (football teams)   food

> I think Barcelona is older than Madrid.
>
> I think Granada is the oldest city in Spain.

11 Writing

Write sentences about cities in your country.

Barcelona is bigger than Granada, but Madrid is the biggest city.

21

2 FESTIVALS

2 We should stay together

should and shouldn't
Prepositions of place
Giving advice
Talking about town facilities

1 Opener

Which of these can you see in the photo?

> a band   a cap   a cigarette   jewellery   signs
> a stage   stalls   trainers   umbrellas

2 Presentation

Read and listen.

GREG   It's really easy to get lost here. We should stay together. Where are Carol, Pedro and Jack?
SALLY   They're dancing next to the band – in front of the Mexican food stall.
GREG   Hey, you three – come here! You shouldn't go away like that.
CAROL   Why not? It's a carnival. We're on holiday.
GREG   You should tell me where you're going. I'm looking after you.
CAROL   I can look after myself. Bye!
BEN   Carol, you shouldn't go off on your own – it isn't safe. I'm coming with you!
GREG   Now listen, the rest of you. Stay together and meet me in half an hour at the YTV stage. It's opposite the cinema. OK? Carol, Ben, come back!

3 Comprehension

Answer the questions.

1. Who is dancing next to the band?
2. Why should they tell Greg where they are going?
3. Does Carol agree with Greg?
4. Why does Ben go with Carol?
5. When does Greg ask the others to meet him?
6. What is opposite the cinema?

4 Grammar

Complete.

> **should** and **shouldn't**
> We **should** stay together.
> You _____ tell me where you're going.
> You _____ go off on your own.
> Why _____ they tell Greg?

➡ Check the answers: Grammar Summary page 110

5 Grammar Practice

Read *Carnival Dos and Don'ts*. Then complete the sentences with *should* or *shouldn't*.

> **CARNIVAL Dos and Don't's**
> ✗ Don't carry lots of money.
> ✓ Walk in the same direction as the crowd.
> ✗ Don't jump in front of a band – follow it.
> ✓ Look after children.
> ✗ Don't wear expensive jewellery.

1. You _____ carry lots of money.
2. You _____ look after children.
3. You _____ jump in front of a band.
4. You _____ wear expensive jewellery.
5. You _____ walk in the same direction as the crowd.

6 Speaking

Read the YTV questionnaire. What should/shouldn't you do in your country?

> You should take flowers.

QUESTIONNAIRE YTV

What should/shouldn't you do when …

1 … you visit someone's home for the first time?
A Take flowers.
B Arrive half an hour early.
C Arrive a little late.
D Take your own food with you.

2 … you meet someone's parents?
A Kiss them once on the cheek.
B Kiss them twice on the cheek.
C Shake hands.

3 … someone gives you a present?
A Say thank you and open it immediately.
B Say thank you and open it later.

4 … you answer the telephone?
A Say hello.
B Say your name.
C Say your number.
D Say your address.

5 … you are a guest at a meal?
A Start eating first.
B Wait until others are eating.
C Eat everything on your plate.
D Leave some food on your plate.

7 Writing

Write a paragraph giving advice to a visitor to your country. Use the topics in the questionnaire and add others.

When you visit someone's home for the first time, you should take flowers.

8 Pronunciation

Listen and repeat.

/s/ /ʃ/

She's got sixty shirts and sixty-six skirts – she should stop shopping!

9 Grammar Practice

Look at the photo on page 22 and complete with prepositions from the box.

1 Tomek is standing _____ Gabi.
2 Greg is standing _____ the group.
3 Gabi is _____ Tomek and Laura.
4 Ben is _____ Greg.
5 Sally is _____ Ben.
6 The woman in red is dancing _____ Greg.

Prepositions of place

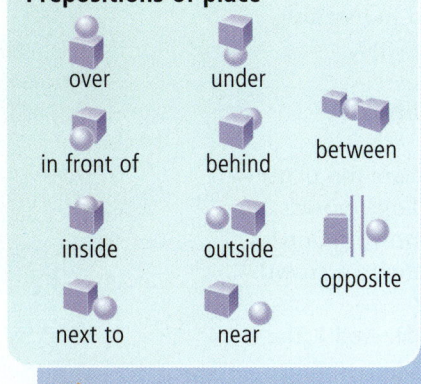

over   under
in front of   behind   between
inside   outside   opposite
next to   near

→ Grammar Summary page 111

10 Vocabulary

Ask and answer questions about the High Street.

> Where's the post office?
> It's opposite the bank.

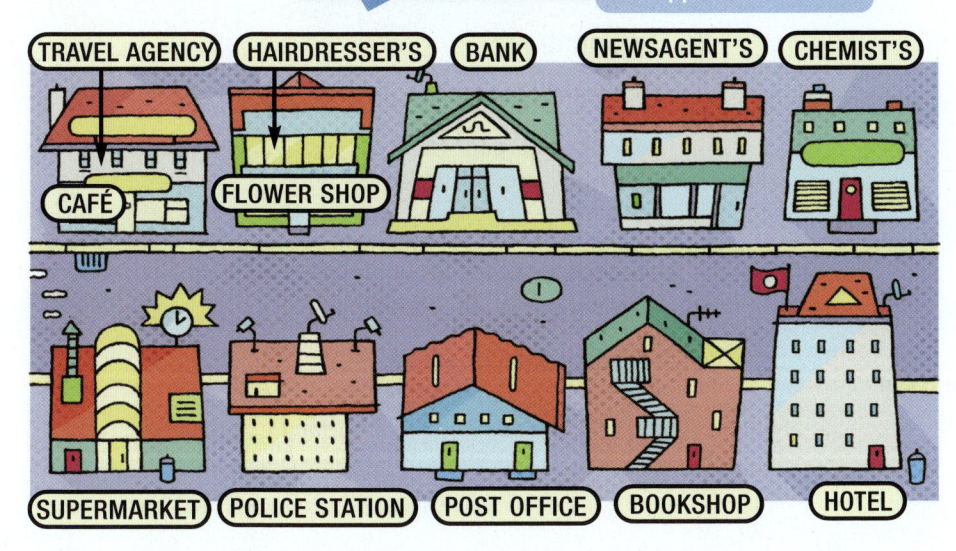

TRAVEL AGENCY   HAIRDRESSER'S   BANK   NEWSAGENT'S   CHEMIST'S
CAFÉ   FLOWER SHOP
SUPERMARKET   POLICE STATION   POST OFFICE   BOOKSHOP   HOTEL

11 Role Play

Act out a conversation between a visitor and a local (someone who knows the street). You can use the phrases in the boxes.

Visitor	Local
Say *Excuse me.*	
	Ask *Can I help?*
Ask *Where can I …?*	
	Answer.
Say *Thank you.*	

Visitor
Where can I …
buy some medicine?
buy some stamps?
find the police?
book a flight?
buy some flowers?
get some bread?
get a haircut?
change some money?
get a cup of coffee?
buy some magazines?

Local
The … is
near …   next to …
opposite …   between …
over …   under …

12 Writing

Write conversations between a local and two visitors. Use the phrases in the boxes in exercise 11.

2 FESTIVALS

3 I love going to festivals

Verb/Preposition + gerund
Talking about likes and dislikes
Talking about ability

1 Opener

Where are Ben and Carol dancing? Which kinds of music do you like dancing to?

> **Music**
> heavy metal   house   jazz   pop   punk   rap
> reggae   rock   soul   techno   world

2 Presentation

🎧 Read and listen.

Ben and Carol are at Notting Hill carnival.

BEN   You're really good at dancing! What else do you enjoy doing?
CAROL   Oh, I don't know. Lots of things.
BEN   What kind of things? Being rude to people?
CAROL   I don't enjoy being rude!
BEN   Yes, you do! You were rude to Greg just now.
CAROL   Well, he's bossy. I'm not interested in listening to bossy people.
BEN   What do you like doing?
CAROL   I love going to festivals – this carnival is fantastic.
BEN   I quite like festivals too, but there are too many people here. I don't like being in large crowds.
CAROL   But people don't notice you in a crowd. I don't like looking stupid, so I enjoy being in a crowd. What other things don't you like?
BEN   Oh, I can't stand waiting for people. And I like knowing where I am.
CAROL   What do you mean?
BEN   I hate being lost. And I think we're lost now!

3 Comprehension

Complete.

1 Carol is ____ at dancing.
2 She doesn't ____ being rude.
3 She isn't ____ in listening to bossy people.
4 Both Carol and Ben like going to ____.
5 ____ hates being in large crowds.
6 ____ doesn't like looking stupid.
7 Ben can't ____ waiting for people.
8 Ben ____ being lost.

4 Listening

🎧 Are Carol and Ben lost? Listen and find out.

5 Grammar

Complete.

> **Verb + gerund**
> I love go**ing** to festivals.
> I hate be___ lost.
> I don't enjoy ____ rude.
> I can't stand ____ for people.
> What do you like ____?

> **Preposition + gerund**
> You're good **at** danc**ing**.
> I'm not interested ____ listen**ing** to bossy people.

➡ Check the answers: Grammar Summary page 111

24

7 Grammar Practice

Look back at exercises 2 and 6, and add the correct preposition.

1. interested ____ sightseeing
2. rude ____ people
3. bad ____ singing
4. listen ____ music
5. wait ____ someone
6. talk ____ someone
7. good ____ playing the guitar

8 Pronunciation

Listen and repeat. Mark the stress.

cinema   competition   enjoy   fantastic   festival
hairdresser   interested   interview   notice

■
cinema

9 Listening

Listen to Paula's interviews and complete the chart for Carol and Jack. Use these phrases.

dancing   going to the cinema   losing things
going to the hairdresser   shopping   swimming
talking to girls   using computers

	Carol	Jack	Another student
Loves	*shopping*		
Hates			
Good at			
Bad at			

10 Speaking

Interview another student and complete the chart.

What do you love/hate doing?
What are you good/bad at?

6 Grammar Practice

Complete with the correct form of the verb.

1. He likes ____ where he is. (know)
2. She's good at ____. (dance)
3. What do you hate ____? (do)
4. Who can't stand ____ for people? (wait)
5. Does she enjoy ____ rude to people? (be)
6. They love ____ to reggae. (listen)
7. Paula is interested in ____ to the competition winners. (talk)
8. We aren't bad at ____ English! (speak)

11 Writing

Write sentences about Carol and Jack using the information in the chart. Then write about the student you interviewed.

Carol loves shopping, but she hates ...
She's good at ...
She's bad at ...

Now write about things you love and hate, and what you are good and bad at.

25

2 FESTIVALS

4 Integrated Skills
Celebrations

New Year Around the World
HERE ARE SOME AMAZING NEW YEAR FACTS!

The **Chinese** celebrate the start of the Chinese New Year in January or February and it is the longest, the noisiest and the most exciting holiday of the year. On New Year's Eve all the children wear new clothes and everyone eats special food. New Year celebrations last 15 days, and there are dragon parades and lion dances in the streets.

In **Brazil**, people wear white clothes on New Year's Eve (31 December) because it brings good luck. At midnight people go to the beach and jump over the waves seven times. Then they throw flowers into the sea and make wishes for the new year. Some people light candles and there are lots of parties.

One of the most unusual festivals is in **Thailand**. People celebrate the Thai New Year on 13 April with 'Songkran Day'. On this day people play games with water and throw it over each other! They also visit their grandparents and ask them for good luck.

In **Japan** most people celebrate New Year with their family. They eat special noodles on 31 December, and at midnight they listen to the bells, which ring 108 times. On New Year's Day everyone drinks *sake*, traditional Japanese rice wine, and eats a special kind of soup. The children get red envelopes with money inside, and everyone sends New Year greetings cards.

On 31 December in **Venezuela**, people wear yellow underwear to bring good luck! At midnight they listen to the church bells and drink champagne. Each time they hear the bell they eat a grape and make a wish. People who want to travel in the new year carry a suitcase around the house. Other people write their wishes in a letter, and then burn it.

Like many other European countries, **Italy** celebrates the arrival of the new year with fireworks. On New Year's Eve everyone eats lentils at a large meal that starts late in the evening and goes on even later. Some people also put lentils in their purse or wear red clothes for good luck. Another tradition is to put a candle in the window for every member of the family.

26

1 Opener

Guess: Where are the festivals in the photos on page 26?

2 Reading

🎧 Read the descriptions of New Year and match the paragraphs with the photos.

Now answer these questions.

1. Where do people eat special noodles at New Year?
2. Where do people drink champagne?
3. What do people in Brazil wear at New Year?
4. What else do people in Brazil do at New Year?
5. Where do people eat lentils at New Year?
6. When do they celebrate New Year in Thailand?
7. How long do New Year celebrations last in China?
8. Where are fireworks important at New Year?

Then ask and answer similar questions.

> Where do people eat grapes at New Year?
>
> What do people in Venezuela wear at New Year?

3 Listening

🎧 Paula talks about New Year in England. Listen and choose the correct answer.

1. What do people often do on New Year's Eve?
   A have parties   B go on holiday
2. What do they do at midnight?
   A go to London   B listen to Big Ben
3. What do they do after midnight?
   A shake hands   B sing a song
4. What do people drink?
   A champagne   B tea
5. What do they say to each other?
   A Good luck!   B Happy New Year!

4 Speaking

Look at the questions in exercise 3. Ask another student about New Year's Eve in their country.

5 Writing

Write a paragraph about New Year's Eve in your country. Use the texts in this lesson to help you. Notice that the texts usually:

- begin by giving the name of the country and festival and the date
- continue by describing food and drink, and what people do
- sometimes talk about children and presents
- use prepositions of time:
  on (*date*)   in (*month*)   at (*time*).

Learner Independence

6 What is your favourite way of learning a word? Order these ways 1–7.

- Writing the word again and again.
- Saying the word aloud again and again.
- Revising the word every week.
- Thinking of similar words.
- Testing yourself once a week.
- Using the word as soon as possible.
- Keeping a vocabulary notebook.

Now compare with another student. Try a new way of learning words.

7 How are your English skills? What are you good at? Assess yourself on this scale for Listening, Speaking, Reading and Writing.

5 = Very good.
4 = Good.
3 = OK
2 = Not sure.
1 = Not very good.

Listening 4

Now compare with another student. Choose a skill which needs more work. What can you do to get better?

8 Phrasebook

🎧 Listen and repeat these useful expressions.

Then find them in this unit.

> Come here!   Why not?   Bye!   It isn't safe.
> I'm coming with you.   Now listen!   OK?
> Come back!   Oh, I don't know.
> What kind of things?   Yes, you do!

Now write a four-line dialogue using two or more of the expressions.

A *Where's my music magazine?*
B *Oh, I don't know.*
A *Yes, you do! Come here!*
B *Bye!*

Unit 2 Communication Activity
Student **A** page 106
Student **B** page 116

27

2 FESTIVALS
Inspiration Extra!

PROJECT Music Festival File

Make a file about a music festival or open-air concert.

1 Work in a group and look at Unit 2 Lesson 1 again. Think about music festivals and open-air concerts in your country. Then choose one to write about.

2 Find out information about the festival or open-air concert:

> When? Where? How long? How many people?
> What kind of music? Who is performing?
> How much does it cost? What's special about it?

3 Work together and make a Music Festival File. Read it carefully and correct any mistakes. Draw pictures or find photographs from magazines or newspapers for your file. Show your Music Festival File to the other groups.

GAME Write a poem!

LOVE/HATE POEM
I love reading.
I love football.
I love fireworks.
But I hate homework!

I love _____.
I love _____.
I love _____.
But I hate _____!

GOOD/BAD POEM
I'm good at dancing.
I'm good at rap.
I'm good at sleeping.
But I'm bad at writing letters!

I'm good at _____.
I'm good at _____.
I'm good at _____.
But I'm bad at _____!

Give your poems to your teacher and listen. Can you guess who wrote each poem?

SONG

Read and choose the best words.

(Sitting on) The Dock of the Bay
Otis Redding

Sitting in the morning/night sun
I'll be sitting when the evening comes
Watching the footballs/ships roll in
And then I watch 'em roll away again, yeah
I'm sitting on the dock of the bay
Watching the tide roll away
I'm just sitting on the dock of the bay
Wasting time

I left my phone/home in Georgia
Headed for the 'Frisco bay
'Cause I've had nothing/anything to live for
And looks like nothing's gonna come my way/road
So I'm just gonna sit on the dock of the bay
Watching the tide roll away
I'm sitting on the dock of the bay
Wasting time

Looks like nothing's gonna change
Everything still remains different/the same
I can't do what ten children/people tell me to do
So I guess I'll remain the same, yeah

Sitting here resting my bones
And this loneliness won't leave me alone
It's two thousand/million miles I roamed
Just to make this dock my home
Now, I'm just gonna sit on the dock of the bay
Watching the tide roll away
Sitting on the dock of the bay
Wasting time

🎧 Now listen and check.

28

UNIT 2

REVISION for more practice

LESSON 1

Look at the chart below and write sentences comparing the three cities.

City	NEW YORK	LONDON	ATHENS
Age	400 years old	2,000 years old	6,000 years old
Population	8 million	7.5 million	3.5 million
Winter	January 4°C	January 5°C	January 9°C
Summer	July 30°C	July 18°C	July 27°C

London is older than New York, but Athens is the oldest city.

LESSON 2

Look at the chart showing prepositions of place on page 23. Write sentences describing the position of people and things in your classroom. Use all the prepositions!

The teacher is standing in front of us.

LESSON 3

Look at the chart and write sentences about Laura and Tomek.

	Laura	Tomek
Loves	swim	take photos
Hates	lose things	fly
Good at	write poems	play the guitar
Bad at	get up early	dance

Laura loves swimming. She hates ...

LESSON 4

Look at the text on page 26 and read the paragraph you wrote about New Year's Eve in your country. Write a paragraph about Christmas in your country. Think about:

food   drink   clothes   presents   what people do

EXTENSION for language development

LESSON 1

Choose three bands, pop stars, film stars or sports stars and write sentences comparing them using comparative and superlative adjectives.

The White Stripes are better than Kings of Leon, but I think The Strokes are the best band.

LESSON 2

Write sentences about things you should/shouldn't do:

in class   in the street   at home

In class
You should listen to the teacher.
You shouldn't throw paper planes!

LESSON 3

Choose two friends or members of your family. Write sentences about:

- what they love doing
- what they hate doing
- what they're good at
- what they're bad at.

Petra loves talking to boys.

LESSON 4

Write a paragraph about what you do on your birthday.

REVIEW UNITS 1-2

Grammar

1 Read and complete. For each number 1–12, choose word A, B, or C.

LONDON CELEBRATIONS

Some of London's many celebrations are very British, but others, like the Notting Hill carnival, __1__ that London __2__ very cosmopolitan.

Up to 100,000 people celebrate the Chinese New Year in London's West End in January or February. There are lion dances, fireworks and stages with traditional Chinese music and dance. It is the __3__ important festival of the Chinese year.

A popular parade with lots of stalls and stages __4__ at Easter in Battersea Park in south-west London.

Tourists __5__ try to see 'The Trooping of the Colour' in June. The Queen __6__ in an open carriage, and watches a __7__ of soldiers __8__ Buckingham Palace in central London.

There are fireworks in Southall in west London in October when Hindus celebrate Diwali, the Hindu festival of lights. This festival is also the start of the Hindu New Year and lots of families enjoy __9__ the celebrations.

Guy Fawkes' Night with bonfires and fireworks is on 5 November. People celebrate Guy Fawkes' failure to kill the King in 1605. Many children think this is the __10__ night of the year!

Finally, __11__ Christmas there is a huge Christmas tree in Trafalgar Square. It is a present from Norway and it is the __12__ famous Christmas tree in Britain.

	A	B	C
1	show	shows	are showing
2	are	have	is
3	more	most	much
4	celebrates	goes	happens
5	should	shouldn't	don't
6	ride	rides	is riding
7	dance	parade	walk
8	on	off	near
9	watch	to watch	watching
10	most	best	better
11	at	in	on
12	much	more	most

2 Complete with the correct form of the present simple of these verbs.

> be chat do drink eat get go
> like phone play speak watch

1 In the evening Gabi _____ online to her friends.
2 I (not) _____ interested in going to the cinema.
3 Laura _____ TV every evening.
4 _____ Pedro _____ four languages?
5 Sally _____ her parents every day.
6 Carol (not) _____ pigeons.
7 I _____ swimming on Mondays.
8 _____ Tomek _____ coffee at breakfast?
9 Jack (not) _____ aerobics.
10 Carol never _____ chips.
11 Ben (not) _____ volleyball.
12 The children _____ envelopes with money inside.

3 Complete with the correct form of the present continuous of these verbs.

> drink hold listen look make tell

1 Kate _____ _____ the group about the YTV film.
2 _____ Greg _____ Kate's coffee?
3 Tomek _____ _____ at his map.
4 _____ Pedro and Gabi _____ hands?
5 The actors _____ _____ a film about pickpockets.
6 _____ you _____ to me?

4 Write questions and answers.

camera/Pedro
Whose camera is this? It's Pedro's. It's his.

1 watch/Tomek
2 map/Carol
3 book/Gabi
4 YTV badge/Greg
5 videos/my parents
6 sandwiches/the dancers

5 Complete with comparative or superlative adjectives.

1 The Rio carnival is _____ carnival in the world. (large)
2 Notting Hill carnival is _____ street party in Europe. (exciting)
3 Carol is a _____ dancer than Ben. (good)
4 Jack is _____ than Ben at talking to girls. (bad)
5 Who is _____ singer in the world? (popular)
6 London is _____ city in Britain. (big)
7 Hotels in Rio are _____ at carnival time. (expensive)
8 The Notting Hill carnival is _____ than the Rio carnival. (well-known)

30

UNITS 1-2 REVIEW

6 Rewrite this safety advice using *should* and *shouldn't*.

> *When you go out in the evening …*
> - Never take lifts from strangers, or get into a stranger's car.
> - Don't stay out very late and don't walk home on your own.
> - Remember to carry a mobile or a phone card for a public phone.
> - Make sure you've got enough money for a taxi home if necessary.
> - Don't forget to check the times of the last trains and buses.

You shouldn't take lifts from strangers …

7 Look at the photo on page 11 and complete with these words.

> behind   between   in front of
> next to   outside   over

1 Greg is standing _____ Laura and Tomek.
2 Gabi is standing _____ Pedro.
3 The group are _____ a shop in Covent Garden.
4 There are some flowers _____ Tomek's head.
5 The tall man is _____ the girl in the red hat.
6 Jack is standing _____ the tall man.

8 Complete with the gerund of these verbs.

> be (x3)   buy   dance   go   look   talk   wait

1 Ben doesn't like _____ in large crowds.
2 Carol is good at _____ to all kinds of music.
3 Ben can't stand _____ for people.
4 Carol doesn't like _____ stupid.
5 Jack thinks he's bad at _____ to girls.
6 Carol doesn't enjoy _____ rude to people.
7 Jack likes _____ to the cinema.
8 Carol loves _____ presents.
9 Ben hates _____ lost.

Vocabulary

9 Complete with these nouns.

> actor   busker   friend   guide
> pickpocket   scriptwriter

1 A _____ sings in the street.
2 An _____ plays people in films.
3 A _____ shows tourists around.
4 A _____ steals things from people's pockets.
5 A _____ is someone you know and like.
6 A _____ writes films.

10 Match these words with their definitions.

> briefcase   candle   chemist's   costume   joke
> newsagent's   outside   parade   remember   scarf

1 something you burn to give light
2 something you wear round your neck
3 when people walk or dance in the street at a carnival
4 short funny story
5 shop where you can buy medicine
6 shop where you can buy newspapers
7 opposite of *inside*
8 clothes you wear in a play or at a carnival
9 people carry this bag to work
10 opposite of *forget*

11 Match the verbs in list A with the words and phrases in list B.

A	B
1 change	hands
2 chat	a language
3 do	online
4 hold	aerobics
5 make	games
6 play	glasses
7 speak	some money
8 stay at	a joke
9 tell	a hotel
10 wear	a wish

12 Find the odd word.

1 cost   band   parade   stage
2 expensive   famous   exciting   costume
3 under   street   behind   opposite
4 carnival   hotel   festival   party
5 newsagent's   supermarket   chemist's   bank
6 rude   bossy   angry   happy

PROGRESS CHECK

Now you can …

1 Talk about states and routines
2 Describe what's happening now
3 Express possession
4 Make comparisons
5 Give advice
6 Talk about town facilities
7 Talk about likes and dislikes
8 Talk about ability

Look back at Units 1 and 2 and write an example for 1–8.

1 *I go to the cinema on Saturdays.*

How good are you? Tick a box.

★★★ Fine ☐   ★★ OK ☐   ★ Not sure ☐

Not sure about something? Have a look at the Grammar Summary.

3 PAST TIMES

1 The fire started at a baker's

Past simple: affirmative and negative
Talking about past events (1)

1 Opener

Look at the picture. Use these words to describe what you can see.

boats	a bridge	buildings
burn	a church	escape
flames	a river	smoke

2 Presentation

🎧 Read and listen to *The Great Fire*.

3 Comprehension

True or false? Correct the false sentences.

1 The Great Fire of London was in 1665.
2 The fire started at a baker's.
3 The fire crossed the River Thames.
4 Samuel Pepys wrote about the fire in his diary.
5 Pepys and his wife left their home on Tuesday.
6 Pepys buried things in his garden.
7 The fire burnt for five days.
8 The fire destroyed 12,000 houses.
9 Most people escaped to the sea.
10 Under five people died in the fire.

The Great Fire

When the Romans came to Britain in the first century AD, they built a town called Londinium – London – on the river Thames. London became the most important city in Britain. But in 1666, the Great Fire of London destroyed most of the city …

The people of London were asleep when the Great Fire started early on Sunday, 2 September 1666. The fire started at a baker's in Pudding Lane, near London Bridge. After many weeks of hot weather and no rain, everything was very dry, and the wind quickly carried the flames to the River Thames. Luckily the fire didn't cross the river, but it reached tall buildings full of inflammable things like oil, sugar, butter and brandy.

Samuel Pepys wrote about the fire in his famous diary. When he got up on Sunday morning, he walked to the Tower of London and he saw houses on fire at the end of London Bridge. The fire wasn't near his house then, but Pepys went home and started to pack. At 4am on Monday the fire was much closer, and Pepys and his wife left their home in their nightclothes. They didn't have time to take a lot with them, and later that day Pepys returned and buried his wine and cheese in the garden!

The fire burnt for four days. By the evening of Wednesday, 5 September, there weren't many buildings left in London. The fire destroyed 13,300 houses in 400 streets, and most of the churches. Some people climbed into boats, but most people escaped to the fields outside the city, and only four people died in the fire.

4 Grammar

Complete.

Past simple of *be*: was/were
Everything **was** very dry.
The people _____ asleep.
The fire _____n't near his house.
There _____n't many buildings left.

Past simple: regular verbs
The fire start__ at a baker's.
Most people escape__.
The wind carr__ the flames.
The fire **didn't** cross the river.

Past simple: irregular verbs
Samuel Pepys **wrote** about the fire.
They _____n't have time to take a lot with them.

➡ Check the answers: Grammar Summary page 111
Irregular Verbs page 127

5 Grammar Practice

Find the past tense of these verbs in the text. Which ones are irregular?

become	_____	build	_____	burn	_____
bury	_____	carry	_____	climb	_____
come	_____	destroy	_____	die	_____
escape	_____	get	_____	leave	_____
reach	_____	return	_____	see	_____
start	_____	walk	_____	write	_____

6 Speaking

Look at the quiz and make sentences using the past simple. Then match them with the people.

He built the first car.

Karl Benz!

7 Listening

🎧 Listen and find five mistakes in the text.

Samuel Pepys was born in Oxford in 1633 and he studied at Cambridge University. His wife was half Polish, and they married in 1658 when she was only 15. Pepys is famous for his amazing diary. He started his diary on 1 April 1660, and he wrote in it every day until 31 May 1669, when his eyes became too bad. He described all the important events of the 1660s, including the Great Fire of London. He died in 1705 at the age of 70.

Now correct the mistakes in the text.

He was born in Oxford.

No, he wasn't born in Oxford. He was born in _____ .

8 Pronunciation

🎧 Listen and write the verbs in the correct column.

carried crossed designed destroyed escaped
invented showed studied walked

/d/	/t/	/ɪd/
designed	*crossed*	*carried*

Now listen and check. Repeat the words.

9 Writing

Imagine you were in London at the time of the Great Fire. Write your diary! Use the text in exercise 2 to help you.

- What time did you get up?
- Who were you with?
- What did you see?
- What did you do?

YTV Quiz

Who was the first?

1. He (build) the first car.
2. He (make) the first phone call.
3. He (be) the first person to travel in space.
4. He (invent) the Walkman.
5. He (build) the first helicopter.
6. They (show) the first films.
7. He (design) the first ball-point pen.
8. He (take) the first photograph.
9. He (print) the first book in English.

1860 - Antonio Meucci
1885 - Karl Benz
1938 - Laszlo Biró 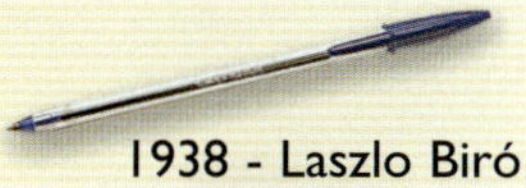 
1826 - Joseph Niepce
1475 - William Caxton
1895 - The Lumière brothers
1961 - Yuri Gagarin 
1939 - Igor Sikorsky
1979 - Akio Morita

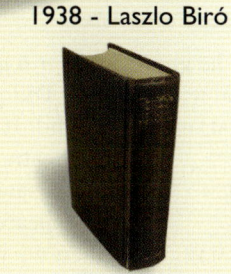

🎧 Listen and check. Then write sentences.

In 1885, Karl Benz built the first car.

33

3 PAST TIMES

2 Did you have fun?

Past simple: questions and short answers
Adverbial phrases of time
Talking about past events (2)

LONDON FACTS

- The old **St Paul's Cathedral** burnt down in 1666, and the famous architect Sir Christopher Wren designed the present cathedral. Building work started in 1675, but Wren didn't receive the second half of the payment for his work until the cathedral was complete in 1710 – 35 years later!

- Christopher Wren also designed the **Monument** to the Great Fire of London. It stands near London Bridge and there is a spectacular view from the top – but there are 311 steps to climb!

- The **Millennium Bridge** is the newest bridge over the Thames. It opened in 2000 and crosses the river from St Paul's Cathedral.

- **The Globe Theatre** is a copy of Shakespeare's original Globe Theatre of 400 years ago. It's the first building in London with a thatched roof since the Great Fire! The first performance in the new Globe was on 21 August 1996.

1 Opener

Read *London Facts* and match the places with the photos.

2 Presentation

Read and listen.

The group meet for a picnic lunch in a park.

JACK   Hi, guys. Did you have fun this morning?
SALLY   Yes, we did. It was brilliant! First we went to the Globe Theatre …
BEN   … and we saw a great exhibition about the theatre in Shakespeare's time.
SALLY   And then we walked across the river to St Paul's Cathedral. We spent an hour there.
JACK   Did you climb up to the Whispering Gallery?
SALLY   No, we didn't. But we climbed to the top of the Monument!
BEN   Carol didn't. She was really lazy!
CAROL   I wasn't lazy – I was thirsty! I sat outside and had a long cold drink! And the others were exhausted when they came down.
SALLY   Well, there were hundreds of steps! Ow! My feet hurt!
CAROL   And what did you do, Jack? Were you asleep all morning?
JACK   No, I wasn't!

3 Comprehension

Look at the photos and reread the conversation. Answer the questions.

1. What did the group do between 9 and 10 o'clock?
2. Did they see a play?
3. How did they cross the river?
4. When did they cross the river?
5. What did they do between 10.45 and 11.45?
6. Did Carol climb to the top of the Monument?
7. Was she hungry?
8. Were the others tired?
9. Was Jack asleep all morning?

4 Grammar

Complete.

> **Past simple: questions and short answers**
> What **did** you do?
> How/When _____ they cross the river?
> _____ you have fun?   Yes, we **did**.
> **Did** they see a play?   No, they _____.
> _____ Jack asleep all morning?   No, he **wasn't**.
> **Were** they exhausted?   Yes, they _____.

➡ Check the answers: Grammar Summary page 111

5 Grammar Practice

Complete with the past simple of the verbs in brackets. Then answer the questions.

1. Where _____ the group _____ at 9am? (go)
2. What _____ they _____ at the Globe? (see)
3. When _____ the first performance in the new Globe? (be)
4. _____ they _____ the Millennium Bridge? (cross)
5. When _____ the bridge _____ ? (open)
6. _____ they _____ two hours in St Paul's Cathedral? (spend)
7. When _____ the old cathedral _____ down? (burn)
8. _____ Ben and Sally _____ the Monument? (climb)
9. _____ Carol thirsty? (be)
10. _____ Carol _____ a hot drink? (have)
11. _____ the others exhausted when they came down? (be)
12. _____ there thousands of steps? (be)

6 Game

Say the past simple. You have five seconds!

> see   saw

7 Pronunciation

🎧 Listen and count the syllables. Mark the stress.

> architect cathedral exhausted exhibition
> gallery millennium monument original
> performance spectacular thousand

■ *architect 3*

8 Listening

🎧 Listen to Jack and match the actions with the times.

9.00–10.00	go to a record shop
10.00–11.00	have an ice cream in a café
11.00–12.00	sit in the park
12.00–1.15	surf the Internet

Now ask and answer.

> What did Jack do between nine and ten o'clock? Did he go to a record shop?
>> No, he didn't. He …

9 Speaking

What did you do last weekend? Think about Saturday and Sunday – morning, afternoon and evening. List six different things, but don't write the times!

I went swimming.
I bought some jeans.

Exchange lists with another student. Ask questions to find out *when* he/she did things. You can only ask 20 questions! Note down the answers.

> Did you go swimming on Saturday morning?
>> No, I didn't.
> Did you go swimming in the afternoon?
>> Yes, I did!

> **Adverbial phrases of time**
> **on** Saturday (morning)   **on** 21 August
> **in** the morning   **in** August   **in** 1666
> **at** 9am   **at** night

➡ Grammar Summary page 111

10 Writing

Write your diary for last weekend.

Saturday
In the morning I went shopping and bought some jeans. At 2.30pm I went swimming …

3 PAST TIMES

3 What was he doing?

Past continuous
Why? because
Describing what was happening
Asking for and giving reasons

1 Opener

Look at the photo.
Where are the people?
What are they doing?

2 Presentation

🎧 Read and listen.

It's 2.30pm and the group are on a Thames cruise.
GREG   The London Eye is the highest wheel in Europe – it's 135 metres high.
BEN   That's terrific! I'd love to go for a ride!
LAURA Tomek, Gabi – let me take a picture of you. Say 'cheese'!
BEN   Oh no, my cap!
SALLY Ben! Help!!!!

Later…
JACK   We were passing the London Eye and suddenly Ben fell into the river!
PAULA But why? What on earth was he doing?
JACK   I've no idea – I wasn't looking at Ben.
PAULA What were you doing?
JACK   I was listening to Greg because he was telling us about the wheel.
LAURA And I was taking photos of Tomek and Gabi.
PAULA And then what happened?
JACK   Greg threw Ben a lifebelt and pulled him out of the water.
PAULA Thank goodness! Was Ben feeling all right?
JACK   Yes, he was. He was shivering, but he was laughing!
LAURA We were all laughing! And I took a photo of Ben because he looked funny!

3 Comprehension

Answer the questions.

1 What was Jack doing when Ben fell overboard?
2 What was Greg doing?
3 What was Laura doing?
4 Was Ben crying when he came out of the water?
5 Was he cold? How do you know?
6 Did he think it was funny? How do you know?

Why did Ben fall overboard?
What was he doing?

36

4 Grammar

Complete.

> **Past continuous: was/were + present participle**
> I **was** listening to Greg
> I _____ n't looking
> She _____ taking photos   when Ben fell in.
> We _____ passing the London Eye   at 2.30pm.
> What _____ he doing?
> What _____ you doing?
> _____ he feeling all right?   Yes, he was.

➡ Check the answers: Grammar Summary page 112

5 Grammar Practice

Look at the photo of the group on the boat. Complete the sentences with the past continuous of the verbs in brackets.

1 The boat _____ the London Eye when Ben fell overboard. (pass)
2 Greg _____ at the London Eye. (point)
3 Ben _____ to Greg. (not/listen)
4 Tomek and Gabi _____ at Laura. (smile)
5 They _____ at Ben. (not/look)
6 _____ Laura _____ to Ben? (talk) No, she _____.
7 _____ Ben _____ to rescue his cap? (try) Yes, he _____.
8 _____ the others _____ the cruise? (enjoy) Yes, they _____.
9 _____ Tomek _____ a photo of Laura? (take) No, he _____.
10 _____ it _____? (rain) No, the sun _____. (shine)

6 Writing

Match the questions with the answers.

1 Why did Laura tell Tomek and Gabi to say 'cheese'?
2 Why didn't Jack see Ben fall?
3 Why did Greg throw Ben a lifebelt.
4 Why was Ben laughing?
5 Why was Ben shivering?
6 Why did Laura take a photo of Ben?

a Because he thought it was funny.
b Because she wanted them to smile.
c Because he looked funny.
d Because he was listening to Greg.
e Because he wanted to pull him out of the water.
f Because he was cold.

Now write sentences with *because*.

1 Laura told Tomek and Gabi to say 'cheese' because …

> **Why?**   **because** (reason)
> **Why** did Sally shout 'Help!'?   She shouted 'Help!'
>   **because** Ben fell overboard.

➡ Grammar Summary page 112

7 Listening

🎧 Sally's brother, Lee, had an accident. Listen and decide: true or false?

1 Lee fell overboard last month.
2 He was sailing with a friend off the coast of Africa.
3 At first the sun was shining.
4 Then the weather got better and there was a storm.
5 It was dangerous because they were sailing in a big boat.
6 Lee called the emergency number on his mobile phone.
7 They were swimming back when the boat hit a rock.
8 A speedboat rescued them.
9 Lee wasn't happy because he lost his watch.

Correct the false sentences. Then write a paragraph about Lee's lucky escape.

Lee fell overboard last year. He was sailing …

8 Pronunciation

🎧 Listen and repeat.

/w/

Why was the white whale whistling when it swam in the wonderful warm water?

9 Vocabulary

Make a word map for transport. Use the words in the box and add other words you know.

> **Transport**
> bicycle big wheel boat bus car
> helicopter plane rocket ship
> spaceship speedboat taxi train

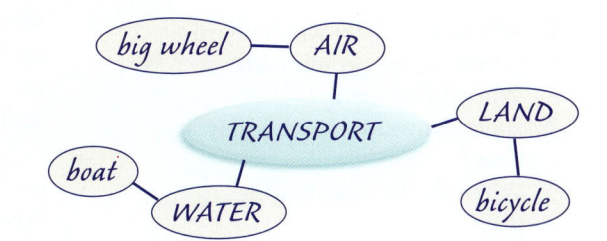

- big wheel — AIR
- boat — WATER
- bicycle — LAND
- TRANSPORT

10 Game

Play *Word Association*.

boat → river   water → swim   fish → chips

11 Writing

Write a paragraph about a lucky escape. Where were you? What were you doing? What happened? Why did it happen?

I was near the station. I was cycling to school. I nearly fell off because a bus stopped suddenly in front of me.

3 PAST TIMES

4 Integrated Skills
Biography

1 Opener

You are going to read about William Shakespeare. Which of these words do you expect to find in the text?

> actor   architect   lifebelt
> performance   play   playwright
> roof   spaceship   tragedies

Reading

2 Read the text about Shakespeare and match these topics with paragraphs 1–4.

Fame and fortune
Later life
Early career
The first years

3 Complete the text with these time reference words.

> after   between   by   finally
> for   in   later   on   next
> soon   until   when

Now listen and check.

4 Answer these questions about Shakespeare.

1 When and where was he born?
2 When did he get married? Who did he marry?
3 How many children did they have?
4 When did he start writing plays?
5 How many plays did he write?
6 What else did he write?
7 When did he die?
8 Why is he important today?

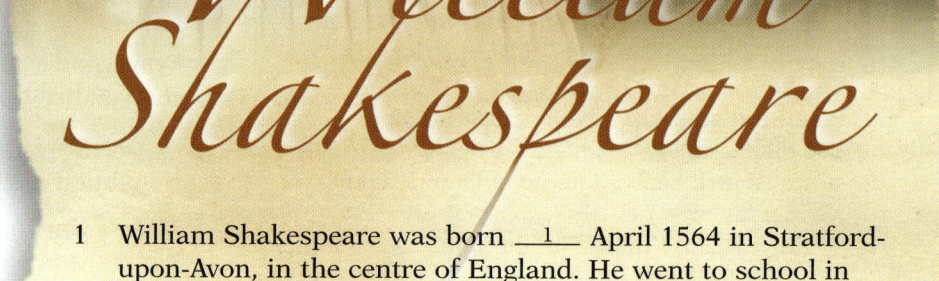

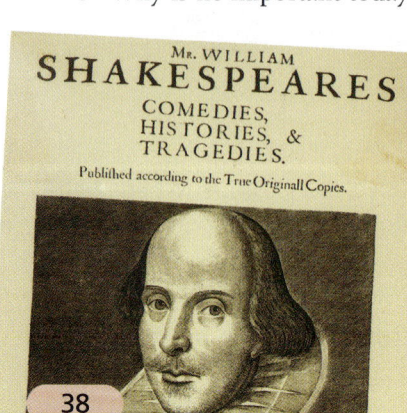

William Shakespeare

1   William Shakespeare was born __1__ April 1564 in Stratford-upon-Avon, in the centre of England. He went to school in Stratford and he probably became a teacher. In 1582, __2__ he was 18, he married Anne Hathaway and they soon had three children.

2   In the late 1580s, he decided to leave Stratford and try to find work in London. __3__ this time, there were several theatres in the city – the first public theatre opened in London in 1567. Shakespeare joined an acting company, and soon he was also writing plays. He quickly became a well-known actor and playwright.

3   __4__ 1589 and 1600, Shakespeare wrote about 20 plays, including *A Midsummer Night's Dream* and *Romeo and Juliet*. His plays were extremely popular and there were even special performances for Queen Elizabeth I! Shakespeare __5__ became the most important playwright in the country. He was now a rich man, and was a part-owner of the Globe Theatre, which opened in 1599. He lived and worked in London __6__ many years, but he often went home to see his wife and children in Stratford.

4   Shakespeare's success continued into the __7__ century, when he wrote some of his most famous tragedies, including *Hamlet* and *Othello*. In all, he wrote 37 plays, and he also wrote many beautiful poems. __8__ he returned to Stratford in 1611, and he lived there __9__ he died, aged exactly 52, __10__ 23 April 1616. __11__ his death, two actor friends collected all his plays and published them in 1623. Today, 400 years __12__, he is one of the most famous writers in the world, and there are many films of his plays.

5 Listening

Listen to a description of the life of Charles Dickens, the English novelist, and complete the chart with dates and numbers.

Charles Dickens

Date	
7 February ____	Born in Portsmouth, on the south coast of England.
____	Family moved to London.
____	Left school, started working in a factory.
____	Started writing stories for newspapers.
____	First novel: *The Pickwick Papers*.
1836	Married Catherine Hogarth, had ____ children.
1836–65	Wrote ____ major novels, including *Oliver Twist*, *David Copperfield*, and the ghost story *A Christmas Carol*.
9 June ____	Died suddenly. Most popular English writer of ____th century.
Over ____ years later	His books are still bestsellers, many films of his novels.

6 Speaking

Ask and answer questions about the life of Charles Dickens. Use the questions in exercise 4 to help you.

> When was he born?
> On 7 February 1812.

7 Writing

Find out information about a famous person in your country: for example, a writer, a musician, or an artist. Make notes about the person's life, similar to the chart in exercise 5.

Now write four paragraphs about the person. Use the topics from exercise 2 and some of the time reference words from exercise 3.

Learner Independence

8 When you want to learn new words, you can make associations. For example, you can associate a word:

- with a picture in your mind
- with a sound or a colour
- with other words in the same category
- with a word in your language
- with a person or a story

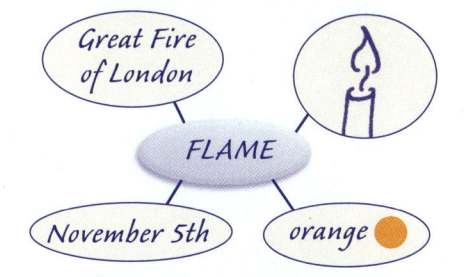

Great Fire of London — FLAME — November 5th — orange

Choose some words and try to learn them by making associations.

9 Word maps are a great way to organise vocabulary. In lesson 3 you made a word map for transport. Now make a word map for jobs and occupations.

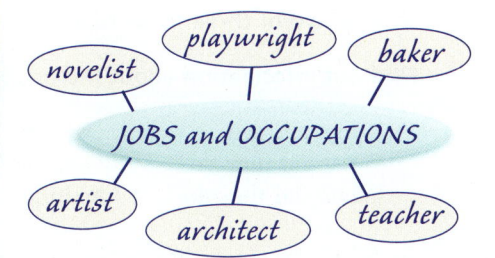

JOBS and OCCUPATIONS: novelist, playwright, baker, artist, architect, teacher

10 Phrasebook

Listen and repeat these useful expressions. Then find them in this unit.

> Did you have fun?
> It was brilliant!
> Ow, my feet hurt!
> That's terrific!
> Let me take a picture of you.
> Say 'cheese'!
> What on earth was he doing?
> I've no idea.
> Thank goodness!

Now think of other situations where you could use each of the five exclamations.

'It was brilliant!' *Talking about a film.*

Unit 3 Communication Activity
Student **A** page 107
Student **B** page 117

3 PAST TIMES

Inspiration Extra!

Bob Marley

Marie Curie-Skłodowska

Martin Luther King

PROJECT Stars of the Past File

Make a file about world-famous people from the past.

1 Work in a group and look again at pages 38–39. Make a list of world-famous people from other countries: for example, sports stars, politicians, or scientists. Then choose two or three to write about.

2 Find out information about the people:

> When and where were they born?
> What did they do?   Why are they famous?
> When did they die?   Something special?

3 Work together and make a Stars of the Past File. Read it carefully and correct any mistakes. Draw pictures or find photographs from magazines or newspapers for your file. Show your Stars of the Past File to the other groups.

GAME Link-up

- Form two teams.
- One team chooses a letter square from the game board. The teacher asks a question about a word beginning with the letter. If the team guesses the word, they win the square.
- Then the other team chooses a letter square …
- The first team to win a line of *linked* squares from top to bottom or from left to right is the winner. You can go in any direction, but all your squares must touch!

C	A	M	R
B	H	Q	F
W	T	P	U
D	L	S	E

SKETCH Shakespeare

🎧 Read and listen.

Two tourists are visiting the exhibition at the Globe Theatre.

WOMAN Look at all these things from the theatre in Shakespeare's time!
MAN Yes, isn't it exciting? There's Shakespeare's computer!
WOMAN No, that's impossible!
MAN What do you mean?
WOMAN Well, Shakespeare didn't use a computer.
MAN Didn't he?
WOMAN No, they didn't have computers in those days. Shakespeare used a typewriter.
MAN Oh, yes, of course.
WOMAN Do you think that's Shakespeare's TV?
MAN Where?
WOMAN Over there. It's very old.
MAN No, Shakespeare didn't have a TV.
WOMAN Why not?
MAN Because he went to the theatre every night. He didn't have time to sit at home and watch TV.
WOMAN No, of course not.
MAN Look at these! Cassettes of all Shakespeare's plays!
WOMAN Did he have a cassette recorder?
MAN Yes, I'm sure he did. I expect he recorded all his plays at the Globe Theatre.
WOMAN Oh, and here's an old telephone!
MAN Hey, why don't we call Shakespeare!
WOMAN Don't be silly! We can't call him.
MAN Why not?
WOMAN Because we don't know his phone number!

Based on a sketch in *English Sketches 2* by Doug Case and Ken Wilson

Now act out the sketch in pairs.

UNIT 3

REVISION for more practice

LESSON 1

Choose ten verbs from page 33, exercise 5. Write a sentence with each verb in the past simple.

Karl Benz built the first car.

LESSON 2

Look at *London Facts* on page 34. Write questions beginning When …? What …? or Who …? about the four places, and answer the questions. Use the past simple.

When did the old St Paul's Cathedral burn down?
In 1666.

LESSON 3

Look at the photo on page 36. Write four or five questions about what people were wearing/doing, and then answer them.

Was Gabi crying?
No, she wasn't crying, she was …

LESSON 4

Imagine you are interviewing Shakespeare's ghost. Look at the Reading text on page 38 and the questions in exercise 4. Write an interview between yourself and Shakespeare's ghost.

Me: When and where were you born?
Ghost: I was born in April 1564 in
*   Stratford-upon-Avon.*

EXTENSION for language development

LESSON 1

Write a diary entry about things you did and didn't do yesterday.

LESSON 2

Look at the conversation on page 34 and your answers to exercise 8. Write a similar conversation between yourself and Jack.

Me: Hi, Jack! Did you have fun this morning?

LESSON 3

Look back at the photo in Unit 1 Lesson 2. Write sentences about what people were doing/wearing and where they were standing.

Tomek was looking at his map. He was wearing …

LESSON 4

Look at the Reading text on page 38 and at your completed chart in Listening exercise 5. Write four paragraphs about the life of Charles Dickens, using the headings in exercise 2.

41

culture
Hello New York!

How much do you know about New York? Try our New York quiz!

1 In 1624 the first people came to live in New York from Europe. They were:
   - **A** French
   - **B** Dutch
   - **C** English
   - **D** Italian

2 The population of New York is:
   - **A** 6,000,000
   - **B** 8,000,000
   - **C** 10,000,000
   - **D** 12,000,000

3 New York is on the:
   - **A** Manhattan River
   - **B** Times River
   - **C** Hudson River
   - **D** Liberty River

1 Reading

Read *The first New Yorkers* and number these events to show the order in which they happened.

A An Italian sailed into New York harbour.
B The English changed the name to New York.
C The Algonquian Indians lived on the island of Mannahatta.
D An Englishman discovered the Hudson River.
E A Dutchman bought Manhattan.

Vocabulary

2 Match the words with their definitions.

1 native
2 forest
3 island
4 explorer
5 boss
6 nonsense

a piece of land with water around it
b something that isn't true or an idea that seems very stupid
c people who were born in the place
d person in charge at work
e someone who travels to new places to find out what they are like
f large area covered with trees

3 Match these British and American words.

British English	American English
car park	apartment
chemist's	cell phone
chips	drugstore
film	French fries
flat	garbage, trash
mobile phone	movie
railway	sneakers
rubbish	parking lot
trainers	railroad
shop	store

4 Writing

Write a paragraph about the history of your town. Use these questions to help you.

- When did people first live there?
- What was the town called at that time?
- What are the important dates in your town's history? Why are they important?

culture

The first New Yorkers

Only a few hundred years ago, the only people to live in New York were Native Americans – the Algonquian Indians. They lived in a forest on an island which they called Mannahatta. Then Giovanni da Verrazano, an Italian explorer, discovered New York harbour in 1524 and in 1609 an Englishman, Henry Hudson, found the Hudson River. But it was the Dutch who came to live in New York in 1624. In 1626 a Dutchman called Peter Minuit bought Mannahatta island from the Algonquian Indians for $24 – today the island is called Manhattan. The Dutch name for their town was New Amsterdam, but in 1664 the English took the town and changed the name to New York after the English town of York.

But people continued to speak Dutch in parts of New York well into the nineteenth century. Many words in American English came from the Dutch who lived in New York. These include: *boss*, *Yankee*, *cookie* (= biscuit), *nitwit* (= stupid person) and *poppycock* (= nonsense). The question *How come?* (meaning *Why?*) also comes from a Dutch word, *hoekom*. The grammar of American English is very similar to British English but the vocabulary is often different. For example, *pants* is the American English word for trousers, but in British English *pants* are what you wear under trousers.

4 SOAP

1 Is he going to shoot someone?

going to: future
Talking about future plans and intentions

1 Opener

Look at the photo. Where are the group? Which of these can you see?

a camera   a chair   a clock
costumes   curtains   drums
lights   a microphone   a stage

2 Presentation

🎧 Read and listen.

The group are visiting the YTV studio.

JACK   Hey! This is where they make *Westsiders*.
GABI   What's that?
JACK   It's a soap, like *Neighbours* or *Friends*.
CAROL Are we going to be here all day? Soaps are really boring.
GABI   No, they aren't!
KATE   OK everyone, in a minute we're going to watch the *Westsiders* rehearsal. After that I'm going to take you on a tour of the studio, and then lunch is at 12.30. We're going to be here all day, and there's a special treat for you this afternoon.
CAROL What kind of treat?
KATE   I'm not going to tell you now – it's a surprise! Now ... wait a moment. Sh! I think they're going to start the rehearsal.
GABI   Look! That man's got a gun!
JACK   Is he going to shoot someone?
VOICE Silence everyone! Action!

The rehearsal starts ...
WOMAN What are you going to do?
MAN   Don't worry, I'm not going to kill anyone.
WOMAN You're crazy! Give me the gun!
JACK   I can't see a thing – move over a bit.

What is going to happen next? Listen and see if you are right.

3 Comprehension

Answer the questions.

1 Where do they make *Westsiders*?
2 Are the group going to be at the studio all day?
3 What's Kate going to do after the rehearsal?
4 Why isn't Kate going to tell them more about the afternoon?
5 What does the woman think the man is going to do?
6 Did the man shoot someone? What happened?

4 Grammar

Complete.

> **going to: future plans and intentions**
> I'**m going to** take you on a tour of the studio.
> They're _____ _____ start the rehearsal.
> I'**m not going to** tell you now.
> _____ we _____ _____ be here all day?
> What _____ you _____ _____ do?

➡ Check the answers: Grammar Summary page 112

5 Grammar Practice

Complete with the correct form of *going to*.

1 Kate _____ take them on a tour of the studio.
2 We _____ stay here all afternoon.
3 What time _____ they _____ have lunch?
4 There _____ not _____ be much time for lunch.
5 When _____ you _____ start the rehearsal?
6 I _____ not _____ shoot anyone.

6 Listening

🎧 Listen to Kate. What are they going to do in the afternoon?

a have coffee with the producer ✓
b watch a film
c watch a recording
d visit other studios
e interview the stars
f rehearse
g act in a recording
h appear on a TV quiz
i have a party with the cast

7 Speaking

Ask and answer questions about the afternoon's plans.

> Are they going to have coffee with the producer?
>> Yes, they are.

Now write nine sentences about the afternoon.

They're going to have coffee with the producer.
They aren't ...

8 Pronunciation

Match the words in box A with their rhymes in box B.

> **A** friend   here   make   quiz
>   soap   tour   treat   wait
>
> **B** break   great   his   hope
>   meet   send   sure   year

🎧 Now listen and check.

9 Speaking

Make a list of five things you are going to do after school. Then ask each other questions about your plans.

> Are you going to play tennis after school?
>> No, I'm going to go swimming.

10 Speaking

Think about your next holiday – real or imaginary! Ask other students about their holiday plans.

- Where are you going to go? Who with? For how long?
- How are you going to get there?
- Where are you going to stay?
- What are you going to do on your holiday?

Now write sentences about what other students are going to do on holiday.

Pavel is going to go to California with his best friend for a month.

11 Writing

Read this letter from a friend and write a reply. Use the questions in exercise 10 to help you.

Dear ...

How are things with you? Are you well? We're all fine here.

I'm really looking forward to the holidays. My friend Carlos and I are going to go to the coast for two weeks – on our own!!

We're going to travel there by train – we can get cheap tickets because we're students. And we're going to camp. Carlos knows a great camping site.

There's so much to do there – we're going to swim, and surf, and dance. And of course, meet lots of girls!

What are your holiday plans? Where are you going to go?

Looking forward to hearing from you,

Best wishes,

Erik

4 SOAP

2 I'll miss him
will/won't: future simple
Making predictions

1 Opener
What are the names of your favourite TV programmes? What kinds of programmes are they? Choose from the words in the box.

> **TV programmes**
> cartoon   chat show   drama
> documentary   game show
> music programme
> news programme
> soap (opera)
> sports programme   thriller

2 Presentation
🎧 Read and listen to *Soap News*.

3 Comprehension
True or false? Correct the false sentences.

1. Robbie stole £10,000.
2. Simon went to prison for the theft.
3. Robbie has a gun.
4. We won't find out what happens in the next episode.
5. Peter James won't be in *Westsiders* after this week's episode.
6. Emma enjoyed working with Liam.

SOAP NEWS

All the latest gossip about your favourite soaps

Westsiders
TIME FOR REVENGE!

The story so far …
Six months ago Robbie stole £10,000 from Blacks, the pool club where he is the manager. But he told the police that Simon, his friend who worked at the club, was the thief. Simon went to prison for the theft.

Robbie, the manager of Blacks

Life in prison wasn't easy for Simon

Now Simon is free and he wants revenge. He goes to Blacks with a small bag. In the bag there is a gun, some rope and a mobile phone.
What do you think will happen next? What will Simon do with the gun? Will he tie Robbie up with the rope? Or will Robbie escape? Or will the police discover them before it is too late? Watch the next episode and find out!

Goodbye Liam!
Liam Swan, who plays Robbie in *Westsiders*, won't be in the soap after this week's episode. 'I'm sure that we'll see each other again,' *Westsiders* star Emma says, 'but I'll miss Liam terribly. We get on really well together and I loved working with him.' And Peter James, who plays Simon, says, 'I'll miss working with Liam too. We had a really good relationship. Now I won't have anyone to talk to in the studio. I hope that he'll keep in touch.'

Emma

Will Simon kill Robbie?

4 Grammar

Complete.

> **Future simple: will/won't**
> I'**ll** miss working with Liam.
> We'___ see each other again.
> I _____ have anyone to talk to.
> What _____ Simon _____ with the gun?
> _____ Robbie escape?
>
> We can use *will/won't* to say what we hope or predict about the future.

➡ Check the answers: Grammar Summary page 112

5 Grammar Practice

Complete with *will* or *won't*.

1. _____ Simon kill Robbie?
2. What do you think _____ happen?
3. I _____ miss Liam terribly.
4. I know that we _____ see each other again.
5. Liam _____ be in *Westsiders* in the future.
6. Peter _____ have anyone to talk to.

6 Speaking

What do you think will happen in the next episode of *Westsiders*? Look at the article and photos on page 46, and think about the following:

> tie him up with the rope   shoot him   escape
> just talk to him   play pool together
> say sorry   call the police   be friends again
> have a fight   have an argument

Then tell each other what you think. Begin like this:
I think that … I'm sure that … I hope that …

> I think that Simon will shoot Robbie.
>
> I'm sure that Robbie will escape.

🎧 Now listen and find out what happens.

7 Pronunciation

🎧 Listen and repeat.

/ɪ/ will	/iː/ we'll
live	leave
fit	feet
it	eat
sit	seat
tin	teen
fill	feel

Now listen and write the words you hear.

8 Speaking

The YTV group are in the hotel. What do you think will happen next? Choose A, B, or C.

> I think Carol will say she's pleased.
>
> I don't agree – I think she'll get angry because she doesn't like soaps.

1. Everyone wants to watch a soap on TV.
   Will Carol …
   A say she's pleased?
   B fall asleep?
   C get angry?

2. Greg brings his dog to the hotel.
   Will Ben …
   A say he's afraid of dogs?
   B say he prefers cats?
   C say he wants to take the dog for a walk?

3. Kate says there's a new YTV game on the computer.
   Will Jack …
   A say that he's not interested?
   B be the first person to play it?
   C let everyone else have a go first?

4. It's Gabi's birthday. Sally gives her a new pink T-shirt as a present.
   Will Gabi …
   A say thank you and then try and change it?
   B say she loves pink?
   C say thank you and not wear the T-shirt?

5. Kate gives Greg a cup of coffee with sugar in it.
   Will Greg …
   A say thank you and drink the coffee?
   B say thank you and not drink the coffee?
   C get another cup of coffee?

🎧 Now listen and check.

9 Writing

What will happen to the characters in the book? Look at the pictures and lesson titles in Units 5–8, and make predictions. Then write a paragraph.

Where will they go?
What will they do?
Who will they meet?
What will they buy?
Will they make something?
Will they get lost?
Will they see something unusual?
Will they lose or find something valuable?
Will they fall in love?

I think Jack and Sally will …
I don't think they'll …

4 SOAP

3 You spoke too fast

Adverbs of manner
Talking about the way people do things

1 Opener

Look at the photo of the group. Which of these adjectives describe how they are feeling?

> angry   comfortable   happy   nervous   sad

Guess: What is Kate saying?

2 Presentation

Read and listen.

KATE   Is everyone sitting comfortably? Well, I've got some bad news for you. YTV aren't going to broadcast the *Westsiders* episode you recorded.
BEN   Oh, what a shame! Why not?
KATE   I'm afraid the director thinks you acted badly.
CAROL   But we weren't acting. We were being ourselves.
KATE   I know and I thought you did very well. But the director thinks you spoke too fast.
CAROL   That's absurd! We just spoke normally, that's all.
JACK   I think it's because we didn't have enough time to rehearse properly.
KATE   It's not just a question of rehearsing, Jack. Actors work really hard – they spend hours doing drama exercises.
JACK   Can you do some of these exercises with us?
KATE   Of course. Does everyone want to try?
ALL   Yes, please.

3 Comprehension

Match the questions with the answers. There are two wrong answers.

1 Why aren't YTV going to broadcast the group's performance?
2 What does the director think about the way they spoke?
3 How did the group speak?
4 What does Jack think the problem was?
5 How do actors spend a lot their time?
6 What is Kate going to do with the group?

a In the way that they usually do.
b Doing drama exercises.
c They're going to rehearse the episode again.
d He thinks that they spoke too quickly.
e Some drama exercises.
f Kate thinks they spoke too slowly.
g He thinks they needed a longer rehearsal.
h Because the director didn't like their acting.

48

4 Grammar

Complete.

Adverbs of manner

Regular		Irregular	
Adjective	Adverb	Adjective	Adverb
bad	____ly	early	early
normal	____	fast	____
proper	____	good	____
quick	quick**ly**	hard	____
comfortable	comfortab**ly**	late	late
angry	ang**rily**		
happy	happ**ily**		

We use adverbs of manner to describe *how* we do something.

➡ Check the answers: Grammar Summary page 112

5 Grammar Practice

Complete with adverbs from the Grammar box.

1 Are you sitting _____ ?
2 Kate thought that the group acted very _____.
3 They spoke _____ but the director thought they spoke too _____.
4 Jack said there wasn't time for them to rehearse _____.
5 The director thought the group acted _____.
6 Actors work _____ doing drama exercises.

6 Pronunciation

🎧 Listen and write the words in the correct column.

comfortably   director   episode   exercise
happily   normally   properly   recording
rehearsal   tomorrow

▪■▪	■▪▪
	comfortably

Now listen and check. Repeat the words.

7 Listening

🎧 Kate explains two drama exercises to the group. Listen and choose the correct answer.

1 In the first exercise Kate tells them how to dance/write/move.
2 In the second exercise she tells them to sing/talk/walk.

Now listen to the second exercise. Guess the adverb of manner before the YTV group! Choose from the adverbs in the box.

1 Ben   2 Carol   3 Gabi   4 Jack
5 Pedro   6 Laura   7 Tomek   8 Sally

Adverbs of manner
angrily   bossily   happily   loudly   nervously
politely   quickly   quietly   rudely   sadly   slowly

8 Speaking

Do the drama exercises using the adverbs in the box in exercise 7.

9 Vocabulary

Match the words with their definitions.

1 broadcast
2 character
3 episode
4 exercise
5 rehearse
6 studio

a place where people make a film or video
b practice activity
c show on television
d practise a play, piece of music, etc for a performance
e person in a soap or a film, play or book
f part of a story

10 Writing

Write a paragraph describing a character from a soap that you like.

- Who is the character and where does he/she live?
- What does he/she do?
- What does he/she usually wear?
- How does he/she talk and behave?
- Why do/don't you like the character?

4 SOAP

4 Integrated Skills
TV programmes

CLASSIC SOAPS

1 ____

Ramsay Street in Australia is the imaginary setting for one of the world's most successful soaps. Millions of people follow the lives of characters in *Neighbours*. Its most famous performer is Kylie Minogue, who became a star in the soap. She played Charlene and Jason Donovan played her boyfriend Scott – Jason was later Kylie's boyfriend in real life. And now another *Neighbours* star, Holly Valance, is making a career as a singer …

2 ____

Hospital soaps are always popular and one of the best is *Casualty*. The lives and loves of doctors, nurses and their patients are what a hospital soap is all about. This soap is fast-moving and action-packed with accidents, serious illnesses and emergencies as well as romance.

3 ____

EastEnders is over 20 years old now and millions of people in Britain watch it each week. Life in Albert Square in east London is never quiet. There's always a fight in the Queen Vic, the local pub, or an argument at the street market, or a robbery. And the characters' love lives are never easy. One famous episode was about a dying woman who decided to do everything backwards. 'It will make my life seem longer,' she said. Soon everyone in Albert Square was copying her!

4 ____

Over 50 million people around the world watch *Home and Away*. It takes place in Summer Bay, an Australian town where the sun always shines and there is always trouble. The first broadcast was in 1989 and the soap tells the story of life in a caravan park. In one episode, two of the characters, blonde Rebecca and dark-haired Travis, left Summer Bay and started a new life on an old sailing ship.

1 Opener

Choose one of the photos A–D (don't say which one!) and describe it to another student. Describe the people and say where they are. Can your partner identify the photo?

2 Reading

Read the descriptions of classic soaps and match the paragraphs and pictures. Then choose a title for each paragraph.

London Life   Trouble in the Sun
Soap Stars   Life and Death

🎧 Now listen and check.

3 Listening

🎧 Greg talks about his favourite soap. Listen and choose the correct answer.

1. What's the name of Greg's favourite soap?
   A Ewerdale   B Emmerdale
2. What's it about?
   A A village.   B A country.
3. Where does it take place?
   A In Yorkshire.   B In the south of England.
4. How often is it on?
   A Every day.   B Five times a week.
5. What was the most exciting episode?
   A There was a plane crash.
   B There was a train crash.
6. And what's happening at the moment?
   A They're looking for a mother.
   B They're looking for a murderer.

4 Speaking

Look at the questions in exercise 3. Ask another student about their favourite soap.

> What's your favourite soap?

5 Writing

Write a paragraph about a popular soap. Use the texts in this lesson to help you.

- What's the soap about?
- Where does it take place?
- What happened in a recent episode?
- What's happening at the moment?
- What do you think will happen next?

Learner Independence

6. It's important to know which words can go together. Match the verbs with as many adverbs as possible.

Verbs
eat   drink   listen   look   speak
understand   walk   write

Adverbs
angrily   carefully   easily   happily
hungrily   quickly   slowly   thirstily

When you find useful word combinations, write them in your vocabulary notebook.

Verb + Adverb   *Verb + Noun*
eat hungrily   *take place*

7. To use a dictionary properly, you need to know the meanings of grammar words. Match these words with the grammar words in the box.

at   boring   camera   dancing   make
slowly   they   to see

Grammar words
adjective   adverb   gerund   infinitive
noun   preposition   pronoun   verb

Look at the Grammar Summary for Units 1–4 on pages 109–112 and find the grammar words.

8 Phrasebook

🎧 Listen and repeat these useful expressions.

Then find them in this unit.

> Wait a moment.
> Don't worry.
> You're crazy!
> I can't see a thing.
> Move over a bit.
> We get on really well together.
> I've got some bad news for you.
> Oh, what a shame!
> That's absurd!

Now write a four-line dialogue using two or more of the expressions.

A Move over a bit.
B Why?
A I can't see a thing.
B Is that better?

Unit 4 Communication Activity
Student **A** page 107
Student **B** page 117

4 SOAP

Inspiration Extra!

Channel 1
6.00 Cartoon Hour
7.00 Breakfast TV
9.00 News and weather
9.30 Talktime with Tracey
      Morning chat show
10.30 This week
      News programme
11.00 1, 2, 3!
      Game show
12.00 1666
      History programme
1.00 News and weather
1.30 Westsiders
      Another episode in the exciting soap – will Simon kill Robbie?
2.30 Murder in Manhattan
      American drama
3.30 Whale Watch
      Nature programme
4.00 Pete the Pigeon
      Cartoon
4.20 Ready to Go!
      Cartoon
4.50 My Teacher is an Alien
      Children's drama
5.30 Here and Far
      Australian soap
6.00 News and weather
7.00 Top Tunes
      Music programme
7.30 Notting Hill
      Documentary about Notting Hill Carnival
8.00 Doctor Lake
      Hospital soap opera

Doctor Lake
Here and Far
Whale Watch

PROJECT TV File

Make a file about your favourite TV programmes.

1 Work in a group and look again at pages 50–51. Look at the work you did in exercise 5 about a popular soap. Make a list of your favourite TV programmes. Then choose two or three to write about.

2 Make notes about the programmes:

> What kind of programme is it? (Look back at the TV programmes box in Unit 4 Lesson 2.)
> Who is in it?   How often is it on?
> Why do you like it?   Something special?

3 Work together and make a TV File. Read it carefully and correct any mistakes. Find photographs from magazines or newspapers for your file. Show your TV File to the other groups.

GAME Word Square

- Work in pairs.
- Write down as many English words as possible, using the letters in the square. You can go in any direction, but all the letters must touch. So you can make PLAY, but you can't make PART. And you can only use each letter once in any word.
- The pair who finds the most (correct!) words is the winner.

S	T	C	E
O	A	Y	A
R	P	L	R
O	E	N	I

SONG

Listen and complete with the missing words.

Do Wah Diddy Diddy
Manfred Mann

VERSE 1
There she was just a-walkin' down the _____, singing
   'Do wah diddy diddy dum diddy do'
Snappin' her _____ and shufflin' her feet, singing
   'Do wah diddy diddy dum diddy do'
She looked good (looked good), she looked fine (looked fine)
She looked good, she looked fine and I nearly _____ my mind

VERSE 2
Before I knew it she was walkin' _____ to me, singing
   'Do wah diddy diddy dum diddy do'
Holdin' my _____ just as natural as can be, singing
   'Do wah diddy diddy dum diddy do'
We walked on (walked on) to my door (my door)
We walked on to my door, then we _____ a little more

Whoa-oh, I knew I was falling in _____
Yes I did, and so I told her all the things I'd been dreamin' of

VERSE 3
Now we're together nearly every single _____, singing
   'Do wah diddy diddy dum diddy do'
We're so _____ and that's how we're gonna stay, singing
   'Do wah diddy diddy dum diddy do'
Well I'm hers (I'm hers), she's mine (she's mine)
I'm hers, she's mine, wedding _____ are gonna chime

Whoa-oh, I knew I was falling in _____
Yes I did, and so I told her all the things I'd been dreamin' of

REPEAT VERSE 3

Whoa-oh-oh-oh, oh yeah
Do wah diddy diddy dum diddy do, we'll sing it
Do wah diddy diddy dum diddy do, oh yeah
Do wah diddy diddy dum diddy do

REVISION *for language practice*

LESSON 1

Look at the conversation on page 44 and the phrases in exercise 6. Write sentences about the plans for today in the YTV studio.

First, the group are going to ...

LESSON 2

Look at the text on page 46 and the phrases in exercise 6. Write sentences about what will and won't happen in the next episode of *Westsiders*.

Simon will tie Robbie up with the rope. He won't ...

LESSON 3

Write sentences about people in the YTV group or your class. Use each adverb from the box on page 49, exercise 7.

Kate shouted angrily at Jack when he knocked over the chair.

LESSON 4

Look at the questions on page 51, exercise 3. Write a conversation between yourself and a friend.

Me: What's your favourite soap?

EXTENSION *for language development*

LESSON 1

Write a paragraph about your plans for next weekend. Say what you are and aren't going to do.

I'm going to watch ... on TV. I'm not going to watch ...

LESSON 2

Write sentences about your next birthday.

- How old will you be?
- What will you do to celebrate?
- What presents will you get?
- What do you think and hope will happen?

LESSON 3

Make a word map for television.

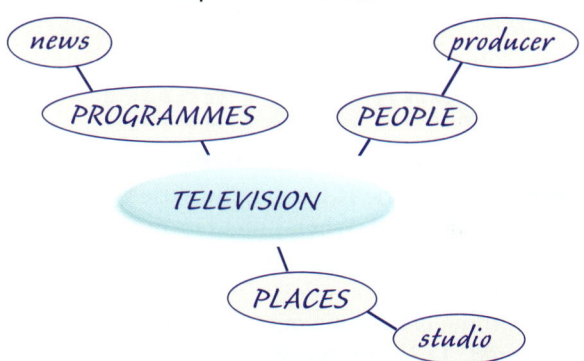

news — PROGRAMMES
producer — PEOPLE
TELEVISION
PLACES — studio

LESSON 4

Write about three TV programmes that you watch regularly.

- What are they about?
- When are they on?
- Why do you watch them?

REVIEW UNITS 3-4

Grammar

1 Read and choose the best words.

HOLLYWOOD HERE I COME!

Is there life after soap? *Westsiders* **star Tamsin Gold thinks so.** She is leaving the series for a new career in Hollywood. When I met her in her London flat, she (1) got/was getting ready for the trip to California.

'Everything is working out (2) beautiful/beautifully,' Tamsin said. 'I (3) finished/was finishing filming *Westsiders* last week and I start work on a film in Hollywood next month. But I (4) will/am going to have a holiday first!'

She (5) will/is going to play the part of a pop star in the movie. 'I nearly (6) didn't accept/wasn't accepting the part (7) so/because there's a lot of singing in the film.' Tamsin explained. 'Everyone says that I sing quite (8) good/well but I'm (9) nervous/nervously about it. I know that things won't be easy there at first, but I enjoy working (10) hard/hardly.'

Tamsin hopes that her boyfriend Nick (11) will/is going join her in Hollywood. 'We (12) will/are going see what happens!'

Good luck, Tamsin!

2 Complete with the past simple of these verbs.

> be   describe   destroy   die   go
> live   marry   work   write

1 Shakespeare _____ Anne Hathaway in 1582.
2 When Shakespeare _____ in 1616, he _____ exactly 52 years old.
3 Charles Dickens _____ in Portsmouth until 1823.
4 He _____ in a factory at the age of 12.
5 He _____ 14 very successful novels.
6 The Great Fire of London _____ St Paul's Cathedral.
7 Samuel Pepys _____ the fire in his famous diary.
8 People _____ to the fields outside London to escape the fire.

3 Ask and answer.

Jack/visit the theatre ✗ /go to a record shop ✓

> **Did Jack visit the theatre?**
> No, he didn't.
> **Did he go to a record shop?**
> Yes, he did.

1 Ben/fall into the river ✓ /jump into the river ✗
2 Tomek and Gabi/have a ride on the London Eye ✗ / go on a cruise ✓
3 Laura/lose her camera ✗ /take lots of photos ✓
4 the group/laugh at Ben ✓ /shout at him ✗
5 Paula/see the accident ✗ /hear about it later ✓

Now write sentences using the past simple.

Jack didn't visit the theatre. He went to a record shop.

4 Complete with the correct preposition of time.

1 _____ July   5 _____ the evening
2 _____ Monday   6 _____ Friday afternoon
3 _____ 5.30   7 _____ midnight
4 _____ 2004   8 _____ 5 May

5 Write sentences using the past continuous + *when* + past simple.

Tom/sail/fall overboard

Tom was sailing when he fell overboard.

1 Pedro/take photos/he/drop his bag
2 Laura/do aerobics/she/hurt her foot
3 Ben and Carol/dance/see Greg
4 Paula/record an interview/the phone/ring
5 Jack/listen to music/he/fall asleep

6 Write sentences using the past simple + *because* + past continuous.

Jack/not see the accident/he/look at the London Eye

Jack didn't see the accident because he was looking at the London Eye.

1 Sally/see the accident/she/stand behind Ben
2 Ben/fall overboard/he/try to rescue his cap
3 Tomek and Gabi/not play tennis/it/rain
4 Jack/have a hot shower/he/feel cold
5 Sally/not dance/her feet/hurt

7 Ask and answer.

you/watch *Westsiders* ✗

> **Are you going to watch *Westsiders*?**
> No, I'm not.

1 Pedro and Gabi/have dinner now ✓
2 the group/do drama exercises ✓
3 Jack/miss *Westsiders* ✗
4 Simon/get his revenge ✓
5 YTV/broadcast the recording ✗

54

UNITS 3-4 REVIEW

8 Write sentences using *going to*.

I/watch *Westsiders* ✗
I'm not going to watch Westsiders.

1 Tamsin/appear in another soap ✗
2 Liam Swan/leave *Westsiders* ✓
3 we/have a tour of the studio ✓
4 Greg/watch *Neighbours* ✗
5 the actors/come to the party ✓

9 Complete this phone conversation with *will* or *won't*.

TAMSIN I hope nothing __1__ go wrong when I'm in Hollywood.
NICK Don't worry. You __2__ have a great time, you know that. And I promise I __3__ come and join you as soon as I can.
TAMSIN I hope you __4__ forget me.
NICK Of course, I __5__ . I __6__ telephone once a week.
TAMSIN Once a week! Why __7__ you telephone every day? You know how much I __8__ miss you.
NICK Because of the 8 hours' time difference between London and California. You __9__ want to talk to me in the middle of the night!
TAMSIN __10__ you think about me every day?
NICK Of course, I __11__ But I expect you __12__ be too busy to think of me!

10 Complete with adverbs of manner formed from these adjectives.

early   easy   good   happy   late
nervous   quiet   rude   slow

1 Sh! Please talk _____ .
2 The bus left _____ and they missed it.
3 Everyone enjoyed the drama exercises and smiled _____ .
4 Carol danced _____ and everyone watched her.
5 Gabi was worried about pickpockets and looked around _____ .
6 Carol spoke _____ to Jack when they were in Trafalgar Square.
7 You feel tired when you go to bed _____ .
8 Please say that again _____ .
9 I can do this exercise _____ !

Vocabulary

11 Complete with these words.

bestseller   building   cast
cruise   surprise   tragedy

1 Last year they went on a _____ around the Greek islands!
2 Close your eyes – I've got a _____ for you!
3 *Hamlet* is a famous _____ by Shakespeare.
4 St Paul's Cathedral is a beautiful _____ .
5 We can't start the rehearsal without the whole _____ .
6 It's a very popular novel – it's a _____ .

12 Match these words with their definitions.

architect   boat   century   exhausted   occupation
playwright   rescue   roof   shiver   whisper

1 speak very very quietly
2 someone who designs buildings
3 what you do when you are very cold
4 very very tired
5 top of a building
6 save someone from danger
7 something you sail in
8 job
9 someone who writes plays
10 hundred years

13 Match the verbs in list A with the phrases in list B.

A	B
1 fall	a go
2 have	a play
3 play	in love
4 rehearse	hard
5 say	place
6 take	pool
7 tie	a story
8 tell	sorry
9 work	up

14 Find the odd word.

1 studio   cameras   lights   novel
2 theft   pool   gun   prison
3 director   cartoon   drama   soap
4 valuable   polite   well   happy
5 doctor   nurse   patient   hospital

PROGRESS CHECK

Now you can …

1 Talk about past events
2 Describe what was happening
3 Ask for and give reasons
4 Talk about future plans and intentions
5 Make predictions
6 Talk about the way people do things

Look back at Units 3 and 4 and write an example for 1–6.

1 *Akio Morita invented the Walkman in 1979.*

How good are you? Tick a box.
★★★ Fine ☐   ★★ OK ☐   ★ Not sure ☐

Not sure about something? Ask your teacher.

5 OUT AND ABOUT

1 What's happening tomorrow?

Present continuous: future
Sequencing adverbs
Talking about arrangements
Describing a sequence of events

1 Opener

Where are the people in the photo?
In a film, on stage, or on TV?

2 Presentation

Read the timetable.

YTV

What's happening on Saturday?

9.30am	Leave hotel and walk to Teen Jeans in James Street.
11–1pm	Watch the filming of a jeans commercial at Teen Jeans.
1.15pm	Have lunch in Pizza Paradise restaurant.
2.30pm	Take the underground to South Kensington.
3pm	Visit the Science Museum with Greg: Ben, Carol, Jack, Gabi. Visit the Natural History Museum with Kate: Tomek, Sally, Pedro, Laura.
5.30pm	Return to the hotel.
6.45pm	Leave for the theatre: *The Phantom of the Opera*

3 Comprehension

Answer the questions.
1 What time are the group leaving the hotel on Saturday morning?
2 When are they watching the filming of a jeans commercial?
3 Where are they having lunch?
4 Who is taking them to the Science Museum?
5 Which museum is Laura going to?
6 Is Tomek going to the Science Museum?
7 How long are they spending at the museums?
8 When are they leaving for the theatre?

4 Listening

Listen to Greg and look at the timetable. Note down *four* changes to the arrangements for Saturday.

Now ask and answer questions about what's happening tomorrow.

> Are they watching the filming of a jeans commercial tomorrow morning?
>> Yes, they are.

> Are they leaving the hotel at half past nine?
>> No, they aren't. They're leaving at …

5 Grammar

Complete.

> **Present continuous: future arrangements**
> Greg is tak**ing** people to the Science Museum.
> We're _____ to the hotel at 5.30pm.
> They aren't _____ lunch at the hotel.
>
> What time _____ they _____ lunch?
> Who _____ _____ them to the Science Museum?
> How long _____ they _____ at the museums?

➡ Check the answers: Grammar Summary page 109

6 Grammar Practice

Write sentences about future arrangements using the present continuous.

they/have lunch/at quarter past one

They're having lunch at quarter past one.

1. Laura/visit/the Science Museum/tomorrow
2. Kate/not take/people to the museum
3. they/visit/the museums/in the morning?
4. we/watch/the jeans commercial/before lunch
5. what time/they/return/to the hotel?
6. we/not go/to the show/tonight
7. you/come/to my party/this evening?
8. I/meet/my friends/in the café at 6.30

7 Listening

Greg is talking about arrangements for Sunday. Listen and number A–E in the right order.

A Have lunch in Camden Market.
B Visit London Zoo.
C Take a canal boat trip.
D Go shopping in Camden Market.
E Walk along the Regent's Canal.

Now complete the timetable.

YTV
What's happening on Sunday?

10am	Visit London Zoo
Midday	
12.30pm	
2pm	
4–4.45pm	

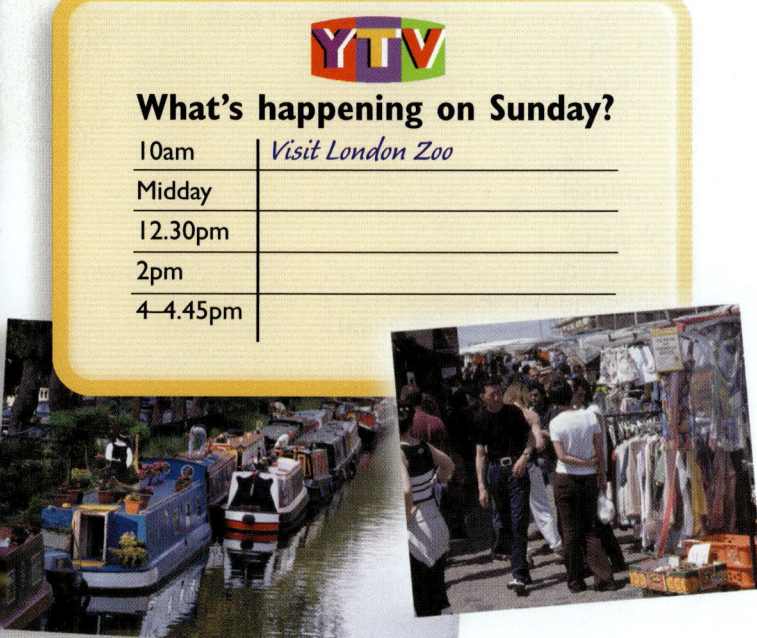

8 Speaking

Ask and answer questions about Sunday.

> **When** are they visiting London Zoo?
> At ten o'clock **on** Sunday morning.
> **How long** are they staying there?
> For two hours.

Now tell each other what the group are doing on Sunday, using sequencing adverbs.

> **Sequencing adverbs**
> **First** they're visiting London Zoo.
> **Next** …   **Then** …
> **After that,** …   **Finally** …

➡ Grammar Summary page 113

9 Writing

Complete Carol's postcard to her parents.

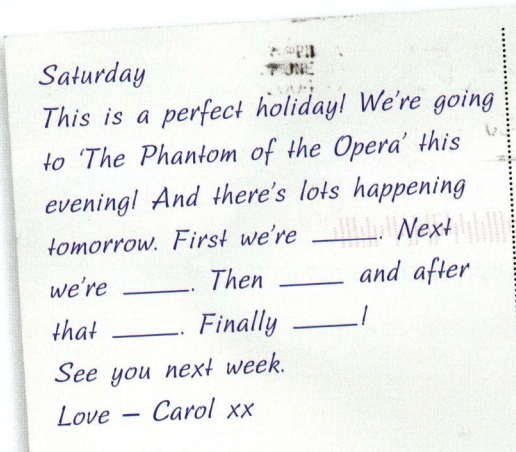

Saturday
This is a perfect holiday! We're going to 'The Phantom of the Opera' this evening! And there's lots happening tomorrow. First we're _____. Next we're _____. Then _____ and after that _____. Finally _____!
See you next week.
Love – Carol xx

Mr and Mrs Sayer
4 North Street
YORK YO1 2QT

10 Pronunciation

Listen and repeat.

/ŋ/ -ing	/n/ in
rang	ran
sung	sun
thing	thin
wing	win
going	go in

Now listen and write the words you hear.

11 Writing

What's happening in your town/region/country this weekend? Think about concerts, sports events and famous people and make notes under these headings.

Who/What?   Where?   When?

Now write sentences.

Arsenal are playing Manchester United at Highbury at three o'clock on Saturday.

5 OUT AND ABOUT

2 You can't miss it!

Object pronouns
Verb + indirect and direct object
Prepositions of direction
Giving directions

1 Opener

Where are the people in the photo, and what are they doing?

2 Presentation

Read and listen.

GREG Carol, are you coming? We don't want to be late for the jeans commercial.
CAROL I'm waiting for Ben – he's on the phone. Why don't you tell me how to get to the shop? I can show him the way.
GREG OK, I'll give you a map. Look, the hotel is here. You walk through Hyde Park to Marble Arch, you go across Park Lane, and straight along Oxford Street past a department store called Selfridges. Then turn left into James Street and Teen Jeans is on the right. You can't miss it!

* * * * * * * *

BEN It's nearly eleven o'clock! Why don't we ask someone the way?
CAROL I'm sure the shop is just round the corner …
BEN Stop, Carol, we're lost! Look, there's a police officer – I'll ask her the way. Excuse me, can you help us? We're looking for James Street.
POLICE OFFICER James Street? OK – go up this street to Oxford Street and turn right. Go across the road and James Street is the third street on the left. It isn't far.
BEN Thank you very much. Come on, Carol, let's run!

3 Comprehension

True or false? Correct the false sentences.

1. Greg is waiting for Ben.
2. Ben is talking on the phone.
3. Selfridges is in James Street.
4. Teen Jeans is in James Street.
5. Ben talks to the police officer after eleven o'clock.
6. The police officer gives them directions to James Street.

Now look at these sentences from exercise 2. Who or what do the words in *italics* refer to?

1. Why don't you tell *me* how to get to the shop?
2. I can show *him* the way.
3. I'll give *you* a map.
4. I'll ask *her* the way.

4 Grammar

Complete.

Object pronouns
Singular	Plural
me	____
____	you
him, ____, it	them

Verb + indirect and direct object
I can show **him the way**.
I'll give **you a map**.

➔ Check the answers: Grammar Summary page 113

58

5 Grammar Practice

Complete with object pronouns.

1 'Where are Carol and Ben? I'm looking for _____.'
2 Greg told Carol the way and he gave _____ a map.
3 'We're looking for the shop but we can't find _____.'
4 'Excuse _____, we're lost. Can you tell _____ the way to James Street?'
5 Ben was making a phone call, so Carol waited for _____.
6 'Hurry up, Ben! I'm waiting for _____!'

6 Comprehension

Read Greg's directions in the dialogue again and follow the route on the map.

Now read the police officer's directions. Where were Carol and Ben when they asked her the way?

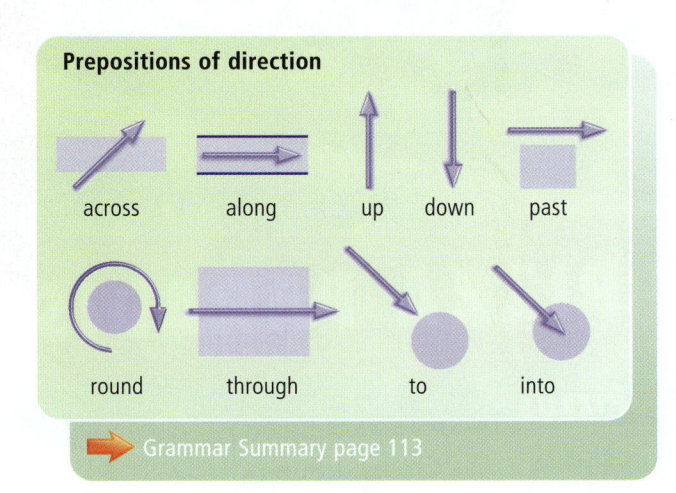

Prepositions of direction

across   along   up   down   past

round   through   to   into

➡ Grammar Summary page 113

7 Listening

Carol is telling Greg how she and Ben got lost. Listen and follow their route on the map.

Now look at the map and give each other directions.

> You are outside Selfridges. Turn right, walk to the end of Oxford Street and then turn left. Where are you?

> Park Lane!

8 Pronunciation

Write these words under *walk*, *stop*, or *go*.

call   cross   don't   four   long   lost   most
phone   shop   show   store   talk

/ɔː/ walk	/ɒ/ stop	/əʊ/ go

Now listen and check. Repeat the words.

9 Writing

Write directions from your school to your home.

Turn left outside the school and walk to the bus stop. Catch a bus to … . When you get off the bus, cross the road. I live in the fourth street on the right.

Now read out your directions. Don't say the name of your street. Can other students guess where you live?

5 OUT AND ABOUT

3 Could I borrow some money?

some and *any*
How much/many?
Countable and uncountable nouns
can/could for requests
Ordering a meal in a restaurant

1 Opener

What toppings can you have on a pizza? Make a list and compare it with the menu.

2 Presentation

Look at the menu and complete the conversation with the names of the pizzas. Then listen and check.

Carol, Ben and Sally are in Pizza Paradise.
CAROL   Let's choose something to eat. I'm starving!
WAITER Are you ready to order?
CAROL   Yes, could I have a __1__ pizza, please?
BEN   What's that?
CAROL   It's a pizza with cheese, tomatoes, olives and garlic.
BEN   Oh, could I have that too? But I don't want any olives.
SALLY   Have you got any pizzas with mushrooms?
WAITER There's a __2__ pizza – with cheese, tomatoes, mushrooms, ham …
SALLY   No, I don't want any meat. I'm vegetarian.
WAITER Then why don't you have a __3__ pizza? It's got mushrooms and there isn't any meat in it.
SALLY   OK, I'll have that. And I'd like some garlic bread, please.
WAITER And what would you like to drink?
SALLY   A cola, please.
WAITER How many colas?
CAROL   Two.
BEN   And can I have a glass of water, please?
WAITER Certainly – coming right up.
BEN   Carol … how much money have you got?
CAROL   About £25. Why?
BEN   Because I haven't got any. Could I borrow some?
CAROL   Honestly, you're hopeless!

PIZZA PARADISE

Pizzas

ORIGINAL	Cheese, tomatoes	£6.50
MEDITERRANEAN	Cheese, tomatoes, olives, garlic	£6.75
TROPICAL	Cheese, ham, pineapple	£6.50
FOUR SEASONS	Cheese, tomatoes, mushrooms, ham, olives	£7.00
SURPRISE	Cheese, tomatoes, spinach, a fried egg	£6.75
COUNTRY	Cheese, onions, peppers, mushrooms	£6.50
Garlic Bread		£1.50

3 Comprehension

Complete the sentences.

1 We know that Carol is very hungry because she says '_____.'
2 Ben doesn't want any _____ on his pizza.
3 Sally wants some _____ on her pizza.
4 Sally doesn't want any meat because she's _____.
5 Sally also orders some _____.
6 How many colas do they order? _____
7 How much money has Carol got? _____
8 Ben wants to borrow some _____.

60

4 Grammar

Complete.

> **some and any**
> I'd like **some** garlic bread.
> Could I borrow _____ money?
> I don't want **any** olives/meat.
> Have you got _____ pizzas with mushrooms?
>
> We use *some* and *any* with both plural and uncountable nouns.
> We use _____ in affirmative sentences, and in requests and questions when we want/expect the answer 'yes'.
> We use _____ in negative sentences and neutral questions.

> **How much/many ...?**
> How _____ money have you got?
> How _____ colas?
>
> We use How _____ with uncountable nouns.
> We use How _____ with plural countable nouns.

> **Countable nouns**
> a tomato   tomatoes
> an olive   olives

> **Uncountable nouns**
> ~~a~~ money   some water~~s~~

➡️ Check the answers: Grammar Summary page 113

5 Grammar Practice

Complete with *some* or *any*.

1 Can I have _____ water, please?
2 I'm sorry, we haven't got _____ ice cream.
3 There aren't _____ glasses on the table.
4 I'd like _____ extra cheese on my pizza.
5 Could I have _____ bread and butter, please?
6 He hasn't got _____ money.
7 There are _____ nice pizzas on the menu.
8 She doesn't want _____ garlic.
9 Is there _____ spinach in it?
10 Can I have _____ more mushrooms, please?

Complete with *much* or *many*.

11 How _____ people are there in the restaurant?
12 How _____ drinks do they order?
13 How _____ money does Ben need?
14 How _____ bread does Sally want?
15 How _____ pizzas are there on the menu?

6 Game

Say 'countable' or 'uncountable'.

> Water.
>> Uncountable.
> One point!

7 Pronunciation

Write these words under *good* or *food*.

> choose   cook   could   fruit   group
> juice   look   through   took   would

/ʊ/ good	/uː/ food

🎧 Now listen and check. Repeat the words.

8 Vocabulary

Make a word map for food.

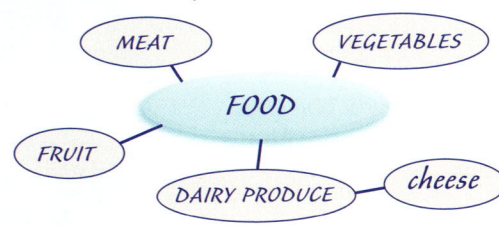

```
        MEAT        VEGETABLES
             FOOD
    FRUIT
           DAIRY PRODUCE — cheese
```

9 Role Play

Act out a conversation between two customers and a waiter in Pizza Paradise. You can use the phrases in the boxes.

> Are you ready to order?
> What would you like to eat?
>> Can I have a Tropical pizza, please?
>>> What's a Tropical pizza?

> **Waiter**
> Are you ready to order?
> What would you like to eat/drink?
> It's a pizza with _____.
> How much/many _____ do you want?
> Certainly.

> **Customers**
> What's _____?
> Can/Could I have a/some _____, please?
> I'd like a/some _____, please.
> I don't want any _____.
> Have you got any _____?

Now imagine you have a restaurant and write your ideal menu.

Exchange menus with another student. Take turns to be the waiter and the customer in each other's restaurant. Act out two conversations.

10 Writing

Write out the conversation between the customer and the waiter in *your* restaurant. Use the phrases in the boxes in exercise 9 to help you.

5 OUT AND ABOUT

4 Integrated Skills
Suggestions and advice

1 Opener

What do you pack when you go on holiday? Make a list and compare with another student.

Reading

2 Read *BACKPACKER'S TOP TIPS!* and match these topics with the paragraphs.

Backpack problems
Tops and trousers
Introduction
How much to take
When it's cold or wet
Not a suitcase, not a rucksack

3 Find the highlighted words in the title and the text which mean:

1. pullover
2. things on a rucksack which go over your shoulders
3. suggestions
4. cloth made from artificial material
5. tourist who travels cheaply
6. does not let water through
7. full of people
8. small rucksack for use in the day
9. takes in
10. (group of) things

Listening

4 Greg is telling Gabi and Tomek about his planned round-the-world trip. Listen to the first part of their conversation and number the countries in the order Greg is visiting them.

Australia   Brazil
Chile   New Zealand
Peru   Singapore

BACKPACKER'S TOP TIPS!

1 Are you going backpacking? Travelling around the world? How many things should you take? And what should you carry them in?

2 Most people realise that carrying things in a big suitcase is a really bad idea. But is a big rucksack any better? Travel writer Hilary Bradt doesn't think so. 'Anyone who has stood on a crowded bus or train wearing a backpack knows how annoying it is. You take up three times more room than normal. And every time you turn round you knock someone over!'

3 So what's the answer? It's called a travel sack. A travel sack is a big bag which you can carry like a suitcase. But it also has straps so you can wear it like a rucksack. A travel sack often has a smaller daypack for things like bottles of water when you go sightseeing.

4 How much stuff can you take in your travel sack? Experienced travellers suggest you first put all the things you want to take in a cardboard box. Then choose only a third of them! And remember, it's not just a question of how many things you pack. You should also think about how much they weigh.

5 Don't wear cotton next to your skin. Anything made of 100% cotton is *not* a good idea – cotton absorbs water and takes a very long time to dry. Get a new polyester T-shirt instead. Many travellers wear jeans, which are strong but also take a very long time to dry. It's better to take polyester-cotton trousers – easy to wash and dry, and much smarter.

6 Many people think that a wool sweater is the best way to keep warm, but wool also absorbs a lot of water. The modern alternative is a fleece. When it rains, an ordinary raincoat is no good because it's too heavy. Take a lightweight waterproof jacket instead.

5 Listen to the second part of the conversation and check your answers. Then tick (✓) the things Greg is taking with him.

> swimming trunks   cotton T-shirts
> jeans   raincoat   rucksack   shirts
> suit   umbrella   wool sweater   tie

6 Speaking

Read *BACKPACKER'S TOP TIPS!* again and look at the things that Greg is taking with him. Then role play a conversation between Greg and either Gabi or Tomek. You can use the phrases in the box.

Gabi/Tomek   **Greg**

Ask Greg what he is taking on his trip.
                                                        Reply.
Make a suggestion.
                                                        Ask why.
Explain. Ask what else he is taking.
                                                        Reply.
Make a suggestion and explain.
                                                        Agree.

> **Making suggestions and giving advice**
> Do you think that's a good idea?
> Can I make a suggestion?
> Maybe you should …
> Why don't you …?
> What about …?

7 Writing

Write the dialogue between Gabi or Tomek and Greg which you practised in the role play.

OR Write a dialogue between two friends about what to take on holiday.

Learner Independence

8 What does 'knowing' a word mean? Which of these answers do you agree with? Compare with another student.

- Being able to understand it.
- Remembering it when I need it.
- Being able to pronounce it correctly.
- Being able to spell it properly.
- Knowing how to use it grammatically.
- Knowing which other words I can use it with.

9 Dictionaries use abbreviations to give you information about words. Match these abbreviations with their meanings below.

abbrev   adj   adv   aux   C   pl   sb   sing   sth   U

> countable   singular   abbreviation   adverb
> plural   auxiliary verb (like *be*)   something
> adjective   uncountable   somebody

Compare these abbreviations with your own dictionary.

10 Phrasebook

Listen and repeat these useful expressions. Then find them in this unit.

> What's happening on Sunday?   Are you coming?
> You can't miss it!   Excuse me, can you help us?
> It isn't far.   Come on, let's run!   I'm starving!
> Are you ready to order?   I'll have that.
> What would you like to drink?
> Certainly, coming right up.
> Honestly, you're hopeless!

Now match these replies to the five questions in the box.

a   A glass of milk, please.
b   We're staying at home.
c   Yes, I'm nearly ready.
d   Yes, can I have a pizza, please?
e   Yes, of course. What's the problem?

> **Unit 5** Communication Activity
> Student **A** page 107
> Student **B** page 117

5 OUT AND ABOUT
Inspiration *Extra!*

PROJECT Favourite Meals File

Make a file about your favourite meals.

1. Work in a group and look again at Unit 5 Lesson 3. What other English words do you know for kinds of food? Make a list of your favourite meals. Then choose two or three to write about.

2. Make notes about the meals:

   What kind of meal is it – breakfast, lunch, dinner or a snack?   What do you have?
   What do you drink with the meal?
   Why do you like it?   Something special?

3. Work together and make a Favourite Meals File. Read it carefully and correct any mistakes. Draw pictures or find photographs from magazines or newspapers for your file. Show your Favourite Meals File to the other groups.

PUZZLE

Read and find the word.

My first is in *theatre* and *school* and *shop*
My second is in *go* and it's also in *stop*
My third is in *left* but it isn't in *right*
My fourth is in *evening* and it's also in *night*
My fifth is in both *food* and *drink*
My sixth is in *hear* and *say* but not *think*
My last is at the end of *day*
And my whole is free time – let's go away!

Choose a word from this unit and make up a similar puzzle.

LIMERICK

Read and listen.

There was a young woman called Ida
who found in her soup a huge spider.
Said the waiter, 'Don't shout
and wave it about!'
So now the spider's inside her.

64

SKETCH The Restaurant

Read and listen.

WOMAN   A table for two, please.
WAITRESS   Certainly, madam. This way, please.

The man and woman sit down. A waiter comes over.

MAN   Can we see the menu, please?
WAITER   Yes, of course, sir. But this table's no good. Much too small.

The waiter takes the table away and brings another, larger, table.

MAN   Now, can we see the menu, please?
WAITER   Of course, sir. Here you are.

The waiter leaves and the waitress comes over.

WAITRESS   Are you ready to order?
WOMAN   Yes, please. I'd like steak and chips.
MAN   And I'd like some fish, please.
WAITRESS   I'm afraid there isn't any steak or fish.
MAN   Well, what is there then?
WAITRESS   Just our special pizza, sir.
WOMAN   Never mind, we'll have two special pizzas, please.
WAITRESS   Two special pizzas coming right up!
WAITER   Here we are. Be careful – they're very hot.

He puts the pizzas on the table and leaves. The waitress comes over.

WAITRESS   Oh dear, I'm sorry. You've got the wrong knives and forks.

The waitress takes away the knives and forks. She does not come back.

MAN   Well, I'm not waiting any longer. I'm eating with my fingers.

The waiter comes over and feels the plates.

WAITER   Oh dear. I'm sorry. The pizzas are too cold now.

He takes away the pizzas. The waitress returns with knives and forks.

MAN   Thank you, but where are our pizzas?
WAITRESS   I don't know, sir. They were here a minute ago.

The waitress leaves and the waiter returns, but without the pizzas.

WOMAN   Excuse me. Where are our pizzas?
WAITER   I'm sorry, madam, but the restaurant is closed now!

The man and woman leave. The waitress comes in with two hot pizzas and the waiter and waitress sit down to eat.

Now act out the sketch in groups of four.

REVISION for more practice

LESSON 1

Look at the timetable on page 56 and write sentences about what the group are doing on Saturday:

in the morning   at lunchtime
in the afternoon   in the evening

In the morning, they're watching the filming of a jeans commercial.

LESSON 2

Look at the first part of the conversation on page 58, where Greg tells Carol the way to Teen Jeans. Write directions for someone who wants to go from Teen Jeans back to the hotel.

Turn left outside Teen Jeans and walk down to Oxford Street.

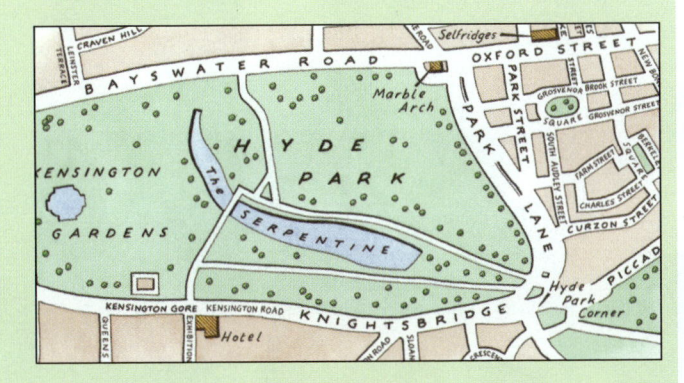

LESSON 3

Look at the conversation on page 60 and at the Pizza Paradise menu. Write a similar conversation between the waiter and Pedro and Tomek. Pedro likes spinach, and Tomek doesn't want any tomatoes or peppers on his pizza.

Waiter: Are you ready to order?
Pedro: Yes, could I have a ...?

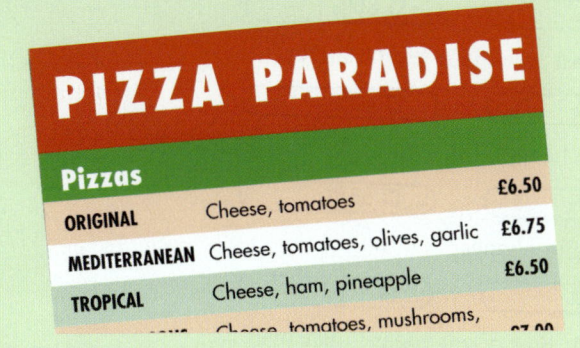

LESSON 4

Look again at *Backpacker's Top Tips!* on page 62 and make lists of items under these headings:

Luggage   Clothes
rucksack   *T-shirt*

EXTENSION for language development

LESSON 1

Make lists of words for places in a town under these headings.

Places to visit	Performance	Shopping	Food and drink
museum	*theatre*	*market*	*restaurant*

LESSON 2

You are outside your school. Write short conversations where you give directions to a tourist who is looking for:

- a place for lunch
- the nearest hotel.

Tourist: Excuse me, can you help me? I'm looking for a place for lunch.

LESSON 3

Look at the word map you made in exercise 8 on page 61, and add at least ten more words to the map. You can also add more categories, such as FISH AND SEAFOOD. Use a dictionary to help you.

LESSON 4

Imagine you are going on a round-the-world trip. Write an email to a friend explaining where you are going and what you are taking. Begin like this:

Great news! I'm going on a round-the-world trip. I'm leaving on ...

UNIT 5

65

culture

TEENAGE LIFE

How much do you know about teenagers in Britain? Try our teenage quiz!

1. What percentage of teenagers think it is important to wear designer clothes? The answer for the total population is 20%.
   - A 10%
   - B 20%
   - C 40%
   - D 80%

2. What percentage of teenagers didn't eat fruit in the last week in a recent survey?
   - A 10%
   - B 20%
   - C 30%
   - D 40%

3. What percentage of 15–24 year-olds say they are very happy? The answer for over-55s is 40%.
   - A 25%
   - B 35%
   - C 45%
   - D 55%

4. How much of their money do teenagers spend on mobile phones?
   - A 10%
   - B 20%
   - C 30%
   - D 40%

5. In 1821 just under half the population were under 20. How about today? Just over …
   - A a quarter.
   - B a third.
   - C half.
   - D two thirds.

What do you think the answers to the quiz are for teenagers in your country?

Girls

Jessie I hate being this age. I do, I really hate it. I'm 15. You can't do anything, you can't go anywhere. Everyone treats you like a kid. I can't wait to be older. I don't talk to my parents about anything important. I mean, I tell my mum quite a lot because then she'll trust me. But there are some things – they're old so I don't think they really understand. We just talk to our friends when we want advice. And there's definitely loads of girls who go on diets when they don't need to. I know some people who get really upset and obsessive about their weight.

Amy I quite like being 15. You don't have any real responsibilities. I think things are quite easy for us. And it's easy to talk to my parents – they're quite cool actually. In fact some of my friends talk to them as well because they can't talk to their own parents. The future? I don't know. You have to live your own life first.

Helen I want to be a model and I've got some photos I'm going to send out after the exams. Marriage? Well, I'd like to meet a nice guy and maybe get married, but I definitely don't want children. My sister's got three kids and she's only 23. I don't want that to happen to me.

Jackie There's nothing to do in this town when you're our age. There's one club and they have 15–18 nights, but that's it. And they're terrible. We spend a lot of time chatting to our friends on the Internet, it's really addictive. There's this disco they organise for all the schools. But all the teachers go. It's rubbish.

1 Vocabulary

Read *Girls* and match the words with their definitions.

1 kid
2 loads
3 upset
4 cool
5 addictive
6 rubbish
7 guy

a lots
b difficult to stop
c relaxed, OK
d man or boy
e terrible
f child
g worried and unhappy

2 Comprehension

Answer the questions.

Who …
1 hates being 15?
2 has a sister with three children?
3 can talk to her parents?
4 knows people who are worried about being fat?
5 thinks the teenage nights at the local club are no good?
6 doesn't want to have children?
7 doesn't know about the future?
8 enjoys being a teenager?

3 Writing

Are the things that Jessie, Amy, Helen and Jackie say also true about life for teenage girls in your country? Discuss the similarities and differences. Then write a paragraph comparing life for teenage girls in Britain and your country.

Jackie says there's nothing to do in her town. But in our town …

6 CITY LIFE

1 Have you recorded everything?

Present perfect
Present perfect with *just*
Talking about recent events

1 Opener

What is Carol doing in the photo?
Who are Sally and Jack talking about?

2 Presentation

Read and listen.

Carol, Sally and Jack are in Hyde Park.
They're making a video about London.

SALLY   Good. Carol is practising with the camera. Now we can talk.
JACK   Look at all those squirrels!
SALLY   Forget about the squirrels, Jack! Listen, why aren't you talking to Carol? Have you had an argument with her?
JACK   No, I haven't! I have tried to talk to her, but she's been horrible to me.
SALLY   But I think that's because she really likes you.
JACK   You're pulling my leg! She hasn't said a word to me all day – she's so rude.
SALLY   I'm not joking. Carol likes you a lot. She's just told me. Sh! Here she comes.
CAROL   I've just worked out how to use the camera!
SALLY   Great! Have you recorded anything?
CAROL   Yes, I have – I've just filmed you two. I couldn't hear you, but this camera has fantastic sound.
JACK   What? Have you recorded everything we said?

What has Carol recorded? Listen and see if you are right.

3 Comprehension

True or false? Correct the false sentences.

1 Jack has had an argument with Carol.
2 He has tried to talk to Carol.
3 Carol has been friendly to Jack.
4 Carol has talked to Jack today.
5 She has just filmed Sally and Jack.
6 She hasn't recorded their conversation.
7 Carol has broken the camera.
8 Carol is going back to the hotel.

4 Grammar

Complete.

Present perfect: *have/has* + past participle
I **have tried** to talk to her.
She has _____ horrible to me.
She _____ n't _____ a word to me all day.

_____ you recorded anything?
Yes, I _____ .
_____ you _____ an argument with her?
No, I _____ .
What _____ Carol recorded?

We can use the present perfect to talk about recent completed actions or events.

I've just worked out how to use the camera.
I _____ _____ filmed you two.

We can use the present perfect with *just* to talk about *very* recent events.

➡ Check the answers: Grammar Summary page 114
  Irregular Verbs page 127

5 Grammar Practice

Write sentences about recent events using the present perfect.

1 Carol/just/film/Jack and Sally
2 she/record/everything they said
3 she/not say/anything to Jack today
4 Jack/be/rude to Carol?
5 they/just/have/an argument?
6 we/not break/anything

6 Listening

Listen to Paula's interviews with Gabi and Tomek and look at the chart. Tick (✓) the things they've done this week, and cross (✗) the things they haven't done.

	Gabi	Tomek	Another student
Bought any presents?			
Taken any photos?			
Done any sport?			
Sent any emails?			
Kissed anyone?			
Had fun?			

7 Speaking

Check your answers to exercise 6.

> Has Gabi bought any presents?
>> Yes, she has. Has Tomek bought any presents?
> No, he hasn't.

Now interview another student and complete the chart.

8 Writing

Write sentences about Gabi and Tomek using the information in the chart. Then write about the student you interviewed.

Gabi has bought some presents this week, but Tomek hasn't bought any.

9 Speaking

Listen and say what has *just* happened. Use these phrases.

> break a plate   open a present   answer the phone
> make a silly noise   tell a joke   have a shower
> send an email   kiss someone

> Someone has just made a silly noise.

10 Vocabulary

Read *Animals in London*. Where can you see these animals?

Animals in London

London has more parks and open spaces than most other large cities. So when you've finished sightseeing, take a walk in a park. You'll be surprised how many animals you can see!

Hyde Park is a good place to see squirrels in the trees and people riding horses. There are also ducks and other wild birds in the Serpentine Lake in the middle of the park. Richmond Park has lots of wild animals, including large numbers of red deer.

In Regent's Park there is London Zoo, one of the oldest zoos in the world, with lions, tigers, bears, hippos, monkeys, giraffes and many other species. The Zoo works hard to protect wildlife in danger on our planet. London also has several city farms such as the Kentish Town City farm, where you can see sheep, pigs, cows and goats.

11 Pronunciation

Which words contain the sound /f/?

> bought   enough   laugh   neighbours
> photograph   right   thought

Listen and check. Repeat the words.

12 Writing

Write sentences about what you have done this week. Use the list of irregular verbs on page 127 to help you.

This week I've played football twice but I haven't been swimming ...

6 CITY LIFE

2 Have you ever ...?

Present perfect with *ever/never*
Talking about experiences

1 Opener

Look at the photo. What are Sally and Jack buying – a snack, a drink, or a ticket?

2 Presentation

Read and listen.

SALLY Hey, cheer up! It's not the end of the world!
JACK I've never been so embarrassed in all my life.
SALLY Carol was really annoyed. I've never seen anyone so angry before.
JACK She heard everything we said about her. Have you ever felt really stupid? Because I do now!
SALLY Perhaps you do like her after all – that's why you feel bad. I think Carol is rude to you because she really likes you ... have you ever had a girlfriend?
JACK No, I haven't! Now let's talk about the video instead. What are we going to do?
SALLY I know! We're in the tube. Why don't we make a video about the underground? In my guidebook it says there's a place called the London Transport Museum. It's in Covent Garden.
JACK OK, let's go there then.

3 Comprehension

Choose the best answer.

1 Has Jack ever been so embarrassed before?
   A Yes, he has.   B No, he hasn't.
   C Don't know.
2 Has Sally ever seen anyone so angry before?
   A Yes, she has.   B No, she hasn't.
   C Don't know.
3 How does Jack feel now?
   A Upset and angry.   B Happy and pleased.
   C Embarrassed and stupid.
4 Sally says ' – that's why you feel bad.'
   What does *that* refer to?
   A Carol likes Jack.   B Jack likes Carol.
   C Jack feels bad.
5 What are they going to make a video about?
   A The tube.   B Covent Garden.
   C The London Transport Museum.
6 Where are Jack and Sally going?
   A To the hotel.   B To Hyde Park.
   C To Covent Garden.

4 Grammar

Complete.

Present perfect with *ever/never*
_____ you _____ felt really stupid?
Have you _____ _____ a girlfriend?
I've _____ _____ so embarrassed.
She _____ _____ seen anyone so angry before.

We can use the present perfect to talk about experiences at an indefinite time in the past.

➡ Check the answers: Grammar Summary page 114

5 Grammar Practice

Complete with *ever* or *never*.

1 Sally has _____ been to London before.
2 Have Jack and Sally _____ been to Covent Garden?
3 Have you _____ made a video?
4 I've _____ felt so stupid.
5 Has Jack _____ had a girlfriend?
6 Sally has _____ been to the London Transport Museum before.

6 Speaking

Ask other students the questions and note down their answers.

YTV LIFE QUESTIONNAIRE

Have you ever …
- won a competition?
- felt really stupid?
- met anyone famous?
- lost anything important?
- found anything valuable?
- flown anywhere?

Have you ever …?
Yes, I have./No, I haven't./No, never.

Now tell a partner about other students' experiences.

7 Writing

Write sentences about three students' experiences.

Wanda has never won a competition or felt really stupid but she has met someone famous – Robbie Williams!

8 Listening

Listen to Sally and Jack and look at the London Transport Museum chart. Number the pictures in the order you hear about them. Then listen again and choose the correct words or dates.

9 Vocabulary

Match the words in box A with as many words as possible in box B.

bus driver, railway line

Transport

A	B	
bus	driver	engine
car	line	park
railway	station	stop
train	ticket	timetable

10 Pronunciation

Listen and check your answers to exercise 9. Repeat the compound nouns. Where is the main stress in compound nouns – on the first word or the second word?

11 Game

Say the past participle. You have three seconds!

buy → bought

12 Writing

Look at the Life Questionnaire in exercise 6. Write sentences about yourself.

I have won a competition.

THE LONDON TRANSPORT MUSEUM

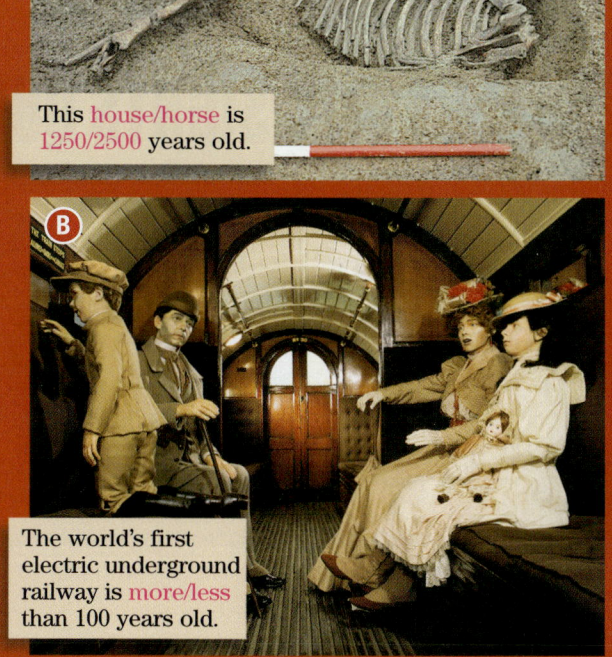

A This house/horse is 1250/2500 years old.

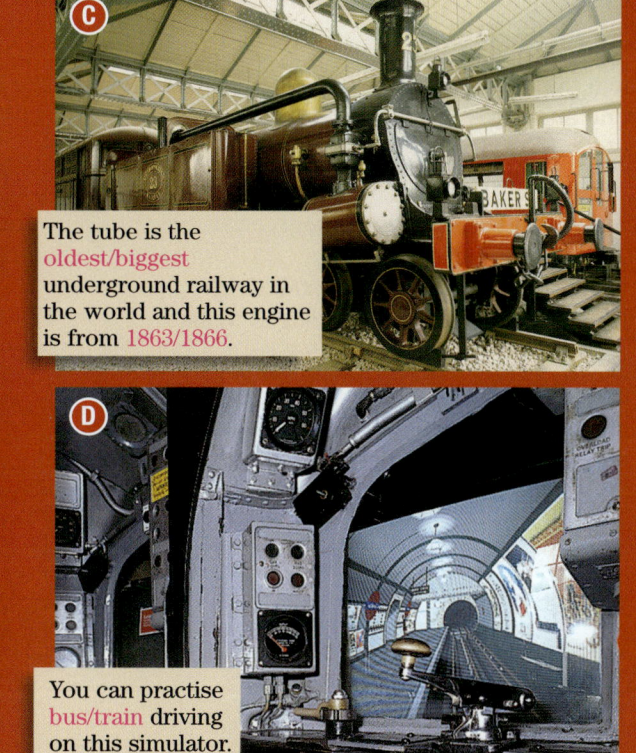

B The world's first electric underground railway is more/less than 100 years old.

C The tube is the oldest/biggest underground railway in the world and this engine is from 1863/1866.

D You can practise bus/train driving on this simulator.

6 CITY LIFE

3 Too many tourists

too much/too many
(not) enough
Saying what's wrong

1 Opener

Which of these can you see in the photos?

> balloons buses churches
> crowds fruit grass a model
> queues theatres tourists

2 Presentation

🎧 Read and listen.

Gabi and Tomek are introducing their video to the group in the hotel.

GABI Hello, everyone. Our video about London is called *City Sights*, and we hope you like it. When people visit London, they want to see all the sights. But sometimes there are too many tourists, too many queues and there isn't enough time to see everything.

TOMEK That's why we've made a video about some of the places we haven't had enough time to go to. We want to thank Greg for helping us – it's his voice you can hear on the video. Please listen carefully and don't make too much noise. Is that loud enough?

3 Comprehension

Match the questions with the answers. There are two wrong answers.

1 Gabi says 'We hope you like it.' What?
2 What do tourists in London want to see?
3 Why can't they see everything?
4 What is the video about?
5 Why do Tomek and Gabi thank Greg?
6 Tomek asks 'Is that loud enough?' What?

a Because there isn't enough time.
b There's too much noise.
c Places which the group haven't been to.
d Their video about London.
e The sound on the video.
f All the sights.
g His voice is too loud.
h Because he's helped them.

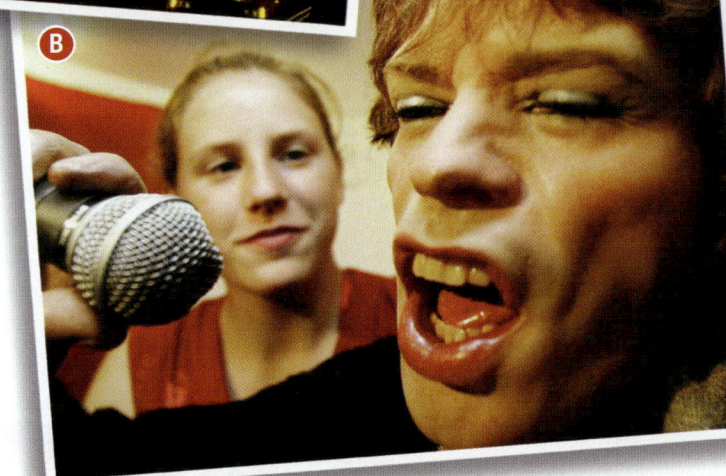

4 Listening

🎧 Listen to the video commentary, and number the pictures in the order you hear about them. Then do the quiz.

YTV CITY SIGHTS QUIZ

Harrods is usually empty/crowded and sells only jewellery/everything/only food.

Most of London's theatres are in the East/West End. *Mamma Mia!* is on in London/Chicago and is a very successful theatre/musical/song.

Madame Tussaud's is near Oxford/Baker Street and is full of models/pictures of famous people, including singers and musicians.

London football teams include Arsenal, who play in red/blue and white, and Chelsea, who play in red/blue.

6 Grammar Practice

Complete with *much*, *many*, or *enough*.

1 There are too _____ visitors in London.
2 Buses move slowly because there is too _____ traffic.
3 Ben doesn't like it when there are too _____ people.
4 There isn't _____ time to go shopping.
5 I think there's too _____ sport on TV.
6 They haven't got _____ money for a ticket.
7 There are too _____ cars on the road.
8 Are you old _____ to drive?

7 Grammar Practice

Answer the questions using *too much/many* or *enough*.

1 Tomek and Gabi are in Trafalgar Square. It's very noisy. Gabi can't hear what Tomek is saying. Why not? There's …
2 Pedro and Carol want to go to the theatre. But they can't because the tickets are very expensive. What's the problem? They haven't got …
3 Ben has bought lots of presents for his family, but now he can't close his suitcase. Why not? He has …
4 Laura always makes mistakes when she plays computer games. Why doesn't she ever win the games? She makes …
5 Greg has satellite TV at home with 54 channels. But it's hard to choose which channel to watch. What's his problem? There are …
6 Kate and Paula need time to relax, but they work very hard and make lots of TV programmes. What's their problem? They haven't got …

8 Pronunciation

Listen and repeat.

/tʃ/ much	/ʃ/ shop
cheese	she's
choose	shoes
chair	share
watch	wash

Now listen and write the words you hear.

5 Grammar

Complete.

too much/too many
They cost **too much** money.
Don't make _____ much noise.
There are too _____ tourists.
There are _____ _____ queues.

We use *too* _____ with uncountable nouns.
We use *too* _____ with plural countable nouns.

(not) enough
There isn't **enough** time.
Is that loud _____ ?

enough goes *before* nouns, and *after* adjectives/adverbs

➡ Check the answers: Grammar Summary page 114

9 Speaking

Describe places in your town without saying their names. Say what is good and bad about them. Ask the other students to guess which places you are describing. Think about:

shops   cafés   cinemas and theatres
churches   parks   markets   stadiums

10 Writing

Write a description of one or two of the places you talked about in exercise 9.

The Café Select is a great place to meet friends. But it's very popular, and when there are too many people, there aren't enough tables.

6 CITY LIFE

4 Integrated Skills
Favourite places

Ben
I've lived in New York all my life. My favourite place is the Statue of Liberty because it's world-famous. It's in New York harbour. The statue was a present from France to the people of the USA and it's over a hundred years old – it arrived by ship in 1885. The statue is 46 metres high and a lift takes you halfway up. After the lift you walk up 168 steps! There are ferry boats to the statue every half-hour in summer, and the trip takes twenty minutes. It's very popular, and there are often too many visitors in the afternoons, so you can't go right up to the top.

Pedro
My favourite place is in Brazil – it's the Cristo Redentor statue on top of the Corcovado mountain in Rio. I've been there lots of times. A French artist, Paul Landowski, created the statue in 1931. It is 30 metres high and weighs over 1000 tonnes. You can drive up the mountain in a car or taxi, but the best way is by train! Yes, there's a little train which climbs up the side of the steep mountain – make sure you sit on the right-hand side going up because the view is better. But when there are too many passengers, the train takes a very long time to reach the top.

Gabi
Last year I went on holiday to Sicily in Italy, to a town in the south of the island called Agrigento. Not many people have heard of it. It's very, very old, and nearly 2,500 years ago it was a beautiful Greek city. My favourite building is the Temple of Concord on the Via Sacra. The temple is from 430 BC and it's the best Greek temple in the world. The beautiful pillars are 40 metres tall. The best way to get there is to walk from the museum. But it's a long hot walk in the summer in the middle of the day! Don't spend too much time at the Temple of Concord though, because there are lots of other things to see.

Greg
My favourite place isn't a building or a statue, it's the Iguazú Falls on the border between Argentina and Brazil. They're the largest waterfalls I've ever seen. They're really amazing because the waterfalls are two kilometres long! Europeans first saw them in 1541. The water falls 70 metres and the noise is very loud indeed. The easiest way to get there is to fly there from Buenos Aires and take a bus from the airport. The falls are very popular, so it's a good idea to get there early in the morning before all the tourist buses arrive. But there's one problem – you get very wet!

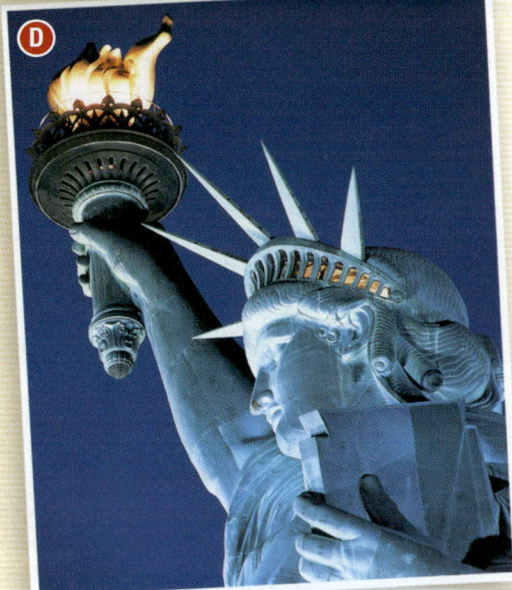

74

UNIT 6

1 Opener

Guess: Where are the places in the photos on page 74?

Reading

2 Read the descriptions on page 74 and match them with *four* of the photos. Then complete the chart for Pedro, Gabi and Greg.

Name	Ben	Pedro	Gabi	Greg	Jack
Place	Statue of Liberty				
Country	USA				
Date	1885				
Height	46m				
Getting there	Ferry boat				
Problems	Too many visitors				

Now ask and answer questions about the places.

What is ____'s favourite place?
Where is _____?
How old is it?
How tall is it?
How do you get there?
Are there any problems?

3 Find the conjunctions *and, but,* and *because* in the texts on page 74. Then choose the correct words to complete this text.

Paula

My favourite place is the Eiffel Tower in Paris. It's on the River Seine __1__ I like it __2__ I went there with my first boyfriend! Alexander Gustave Eiffel designed the 324-metre-high tower for an exhibition in 1889 __3__ it's the best-known monument in the world. It was also the tallest monument in the world until 1930 when they built the Chrysler Building in New York. __4__ the real reason so many tourists go to the Eiffel Tower is __5__ there's a fantastic view from the top. You can take a lift up the tower __6__ see the whole of Paris. You can also walk up to the top, __7__ that's hard work __8__ there are 1665 steps! It's a good idea to go up the tower early in the morning when it's quiet __9__ the queues get very long – there are six million visitors every year!

4 Listening

Listen to Jack talking about his favourite place. Find the photo on page 74 and make notes to complete the chart in exercise 2 for Jack.

5 Speaking

Look at the questions in exercise 2. Ask another student about their favourite place.

6 Writing

Think about your favourite place. Write a paragraph describing it. Use the texts in this lesson to help you.

Learner Independence

7 Working with other students outside class is a good way to improve your English. You can talk to each other in English or play games like this word race.

> **WORD RACE RULES**
> 1 Play with another student.
> 2 Choose a topic (like Transport, Food or Animals).
> 3 Write down as many words as you can about the topic in one minute.
> 4 Who has the most words?

You can also play this game with grammar, for example, prepositions, adjectives or adverbs.

8 How good a language learner are you? Assess yourself and then ask another student to assess you.

How good are you at …?
understanding grammar
increasing vocabulary
using a dictionary
working with other students
listening to others
doing homework

5 = Very good.
4 = Good.
3 = OK
2 = Not sure.
1 = Not very good.

Now compare your scores with your partner's assessment of you. Are there any differences? What are you going to do about them?

9 Phrasebook

Listen and repeat these useful expressions.
Then find them in this unit.

> You're pulling my leg!   I'm not joking.
> Here she comes.   Hey, cheer up!
> It's not the end of the world!
> What are we going to do?   Why don't we …?
> OK. Let's go there then.
> But there's one problem …

Which expression:

a is something you say to someone who is unhappy?
b is a reply to something very surprising?
c shows that you agree?
d is a suggestion?

Unit 6 Communication Activity
Student **A** page 108
Student **B** page 118

75

6 CITY LIFE
Inspiration Extra!

PROJECT Town Centre File
Make a file about your town centre.

1 Work in a group and look again at pages 74–75. Then look back at page 73, exercise 9. What other English words do you know for shops and places?

2 Think about the centre of your town. Make a list of the shops and other buildings and make notes about them:

> Name   Where is it?   Telephone
> When is it open?   What can you do/buy there?
> Something special about your town centre?

3 Work together and make a Town Centre File. Draw a map and write a description of the area. Read it carefully and correct any mistakes. Show your Town Centre File to the other groups.

GAME Alphabet Poem
Write an alphabet poem. Use the list of irregular verbs on page 127 to help you.

Things I've done …
I've …
Answered lots of questions
Been to Brazil
Climbed a lot of hills
Done my homework and
Eaten a lot of meals
Found a friend
Given her a present
Had a haircut and
Ironed my jacket
Just sung a song
Kept a notebook
Lost some money
Made some mistakes
Often been happy
Played lots of games
Quickly and slowly
Read a hundred books and
Seen fifty films
Tried to play tennis and
Usually lost
Visited London
What a lot to see!
X is too difficult
You know and so is
Z

Give your poems to your teacher and listen. Can you guess who wrote each poem?

SONG
Read and try to guess the missing words.
Then listen and check.

Blowin' In The Wind
Bob Dylan

How many roads must a man walk down
Before you call him a man?
Yes, and how ___1___ seas must a white dove sail
Before she sleeps in the sand?
Yes, and how many times must the cannon balls fly
___2___ they're forever banned?
The answer, my friend, is blowin' in the wind,
The answer is blowin' in the wind

How many times must a man look up
Before he can ___3___ the sky?
Yes, and how many ears must one man have
Before he can ___4___ people cry?
Yes, and how many deaths will it take till he knows
That too many ___5___ have died?
The answer, my friend, is blowin' in the wind,
The answer is blowin' in the wind

How many years can a mountain exist
Before it is washed to the sea?
Yes, and how many years can some people exist
Before they're allowed to be ___6___?
And how many times can a man turn his head
And pretend that ___7___ just doesn't see?
The answer, my friend, is blowin' in the wind,
The answer is blowin' in the wind

76

UNIT 6

REVISION *for more practice*

LESSON 1

Write sentences about the YTV group's time in London. Look back at Units 1–6, and use some of these phrases.

> visit Covent Garden   visit Trafalgar Square
> watch a football match   meet David Beckham
> watch buskers   see The Trooping of the Colour
> go for a ride on the London Eye
> walk around the Westsiders studio
> act in a soap on TV

They've visited Covent Garden and Trafalgar Square. They haven't ...

LESSON 2

Write five questions beginning *Have you ever ... ?* using these verbs.

> made   been (to)   read   seen   played

Have you ever made a cake?

Now answer the questions for yourself.

No, I haven't./I've never made a cake.
Or *Yes, I've made lots of cakes!*

LESSON 3

Some people can't stand big cities. Why not? Write three sentences using *too much* and three sentences using *too many*.

There's too much noise.

LESSON 4

Write questions and answers about a place in your country.

Where is ... ? It's in ...   What's it like? It's ...

EXTENSION *for language development*

LESSON 1

Write five sentences about things you have done this week, and five sentences about things you haven't done this week.

I've played tennis twice.
I haven't watched a football match.

LESSON 2

Read what happened to Kate's sister, Jenny. Then look at the Life Questionnaire on page 71, exercise 6, and write an interview between a YTV magazine reporter and Jenny.

Jenny Dixon won a painting competition last year, and the prize was a weekend in New York. On the plane, she sat next to a man wearing sunglasses – it was Sting! But when she arrived in New York, she couldn't find her passport and she took the next plane home!

Reporter: Have you ever won a competition?
Jenny: Yes, I have. I won a painting competition last year.

LESSON 3

Think about your town, or a large town in your region. Write a paragraph giving suggestions to a visitor.

- Where's the best place to go shopping?
- Which sports teams can you see?
- What can you do in the evenings?

One of the most popular shops in my town is ...

LESSON 4

Beautiful places often have too many tourists. Write a description of a beautiful place which has too many tourists.

77

REVIEW UNITS 5-6

Grammar

1 Read and complete. For each number 1–10, choose word A, B, or C.

No singer has had a career like Kylie Minogue and no one __1__ to more people at the same time. __2__ the Sydney Olympic Games in 2000 she sang *Dancing Queen* to a worldwide TV audience of four *billion* people.

Today she is one of the most successful singers the world has __3__ seen, but she started performing as a child actor in soaps on Australian TV.

Kylie Ann Minogue was born in Melbourne, Australia, on 28 May 1968. Her first TV role came when she __4__ only twelve years old, and six years later she left school and joined *Neighbours*.

A year later, her first single, *Locomotion*, was a Number One hit in Australia. But it was the next song, *I Should Be So Lucky*, released in January 1988, which made __5__ a world star. It was the biggest-selling single in the UK that year. 'A new star __6__ arrived,' the newspapers said. 'It's the first time a singer has __7__ had a Number One in the UK and Australia at the same time.'

Now Kylie has had over forty hit singles around the world. She __8__ hundreds of awards and is a household name everywhere. But Kylie herself __9__ changed. Ask her how many records she has sold or how __10__ money she has, and she smiles her famous smile. She simply enjoys making people happy and they love her for being herself.

1	A sang	B sung	C has sung
2	A At	B In	C On
3	A always	B ever	C never
4	A has been	B is	C was
5	A her	B her's	C she
6	A have	B has	C had
7	A before	B ever	C never
8	A has won	B wins	C won
9	A hasn't	B doesn't	C wasn't
10	A any	B many	C much

2 Ask Kate questions about future arrangements. Listen to the answers and write the dates.

Gabi/return to Switzerland

> When is she returning to Switzerland?

On 31 August.

1 Gabi/return to Switzerland *31 August*.
2 Pedro/fly home
3 Laura and Sally/visit Scotland
4 Tomek/go on holiday
5 Carol and Jack/go back to school
6 you/get married

Now write sentences.

1 Gabi is returning to Switzerland on 31st August.

3 Ben is talking to Sally about Saturday morning. Complete with object pronouns.

'This morning, some friends called me from Scotland. I was talking to __1__ on the phone and Carol was waiting for __2__. So Greg gave Carol a map of central London and told __3__ the way to Teen Jeans. But I don't think Carol listened to __4__! We looked for Teen Jeans but we couldn't find __5__, so we asked a police officer to help __6__. When we ran into the shop, you were all waiting for __7__. It was great to see __8__! And we were just in time for the commercial – I'm glad I didn't miss __9__.'

4 Complete with these prepositions.

> across along down into
> past through to up

The River Seine runs __1__ the centre of Paris and there are many famous buildings and attractions __2__ the river. You can take a boat trip __3__ the Eiffel Tower, the Louvre, and Notre Dame Cathedral. But don't fall __4__ the river!

There are lots of bridges over the Seine. Paula and her boyfriend walked __5__ a bridge to the Eiffel Tower. She took a lift __6__ the top of the tower, but her boyfriend climbed __7__ the steps! He couldn't walk __8__ the steps because he was exhausted – he took the lift down with Paula!

5 Choose *some* or *any*.

1 I want to buy some/any presents for my family.
2 Could you lend me some/any money for an ice cream?
3 There aren't some/any empty tables in the café.
4 Would you like some/any water with your meal?
5 I haven't got some/any expensive jewellery.
6 Do you sell some/any French newspapers?

6 Complete with *How much/many*, and write the answers.

1 ____ ____ water do you drink every day?
2 ____ ____ meals do you have every day?
3 ____ ____ money do you spend every week?
4 ____ ____ books do you read every month?
5 ____ ____ English words do you learn every week?
6 ____ ____ time do you spend at school every week?
7 ____ ____ sleep do you have every night?
8 ____ ____ times do you wash your hair every week?

7 Write sentences about what's happened this week.

Jack/play football ✓/tennis ✗
Jack has played football, but he hasn't played tennis.

1 Ben/speak to his father ✓/mother ✗
2 Gabi and Laura/have a letter ✗/an email ✓
3 Greg/eat a pizza ✗/spaghetti ✓
4 Pedro/dance with Carol ✓/Sally ✗
5 Jack/buy a CD ✗/a book ✓
6 Sally/write a postcard ✓/a letter ✗
7 Carol/break a cassette ✓/the camera ✗
8 we/go to the cinema ✗/theatre ✓

78

UNITS 5-6 REVIEW

8 Rewrite the sentences using the present perfect with *just*.

Greg had lunch half an hour ago.
Greg has just had lunch.

1 Laura had a shower ten minutes ago.
2 Pedro bought some new trainers yesterday.
3 Gabi went to bed five minutes ago.
4 Jack sent an email a few seconds ago.
5 Tomek and Gabi showed their video an hour ago.
6 Kate recorded a programme this morning.

9 Ask and answer.

Carol/see the Iguazú Falls ✗

Has Carol ever seen the Iguazú Falls?
No, she hasn't.

1 Sally/made a video before ✗
2 Kate/visit New York ✓
3 Pedro and Gabi/be on TV ✓
4 Laura/meet Eminem ✗
5 Ben/win a competition ✓
6 Jack/be so embarrassed ✗
7 Gabi and Tomek/see the Queen? ✗
8 Paula/go to Italy? ✓

Now write sentences.

Carol has never seen the Iguazú Falls.

10 Complete with *much*, *many* or *enough* and write the answers.

1 Are there too _____ tourists in your town?
2 Is there too _____ traffic in the streets?
3 Have you spent too _____ money this week?
4 Have you watched too _____ TV programmes this week?
5 Have you got too _____ TV channels?
6 Have you got too _____ homework?
7 Do you always have _____ sleep?
8 Do you go to bed early _____?

Vocabulary

11 Complete with these words.

breakfast   customer   guidebook   menu
park   producer   stadium   tie   waiter

1 A _____ is someone who works in a restaurant.
2 A _____ is someone who is in charge of a film.
3 A _____ is someone who buys things in a shop or a meal in a restaurant.
4 A _____ is a list of the food you can order in a restaurant.
5 A _____ is a green open space in a town or city.
6 A _____ is something that a man wears round his neck over a shirt.
7 A _____ tells tourists about a place they are visiting.
8 A _____ is a place where they play football.
9 _____ is the first meal of the day.

12 Match these words with their definitions.

annoyed   commercial   dairy produce   market
pillar   queue   rude   starving   stupid   vegetarian

1 tall column which holds up a roof or bridge
2 something you watch on TV
3 very very hungry
4 someone who doesn't eat meat
5 butter and cheese, for example
6 place (often outside) where you can buy things from stalls
7 opposite of *polite*
8 quite angry
9 opposite of *clever*
10 line of people waiting for something

13 Match the verbs in list A with the phrases in list B.

A	B
1 cross	a competition
2 feel	a meal
3 give	a lot of noise
4 go	directions
5 make	embarrassed
6 order	shopping
7 pull	someone's leg
8 show	someone the way
9 visit	the road
10 win	the zoo

14 Find the odd word.

1 canal   river   market   sea
2 hotel   museum   theatre   statue
3 annoyed   embarrassed   friendly   upset
4 parks   goats   pigs   cows
5 film   model   screen   cinema

PROGRESS CHECK

Now you can...

1 Talk about future arrangements
2 Describe a sequence of events
3 Give directions
4 Order a meal in a restaurant
5 Make suggestions and give advice
6 Talk about very recent events
7 Talk about experiences
8 Say what's wrong with something

Look back at Units 5 and 6 and write an example for 1–8.

1 *We're meeting tomorrow at 12.*

How good are you? Tick a box.

★★★ Fine ☐   ★★ OK ☐   ★ Not sure ☐

Not sure about something? Ask another student.

7 WONDERFUL WORLD

1 They must eat insects and worms
must and *mustn't*
Expressing obligation and prohibition

I'm A Celebrity – Get Me Out Of Here!

I'm A Celebrity – Get Me Out Of Here! is a very popular 'reality' TV show. The celebrities who take part in the programme must give up luxuries and spend up to a fortnight in a camp in the Australian jungle. During that time, hidden cameras film everything they do and say, day and night.

Each person can take one 'luxury item', such as a hat, a notebook, or even make-up – but they mustn't take things like mobile phones. The group gets basic supplies: two knives, three spoons, 10 boxes of matches, candles, a chopping board, shampoo, toilet paper, a mirror, paraffin, a cooking pot, and rice and beans. At the centre of the camp is a log fire, and the celebrities must prepare and cook their own food. And they mustn't forget the dangers of the jungle – there are poisonous snakes and spiders in the area! Before they go, they must learn basic survival techniques, such as emergency treatment of snake bites.

In the first week, the celebrities must do different things to win extra food – the TV viewers choose who does the task each day. What kind of things must the contestants do? For example, they must eat insects and worms, or carry live snakes, or spend the whole night alone in the jungle. One person had to walk through water full of crocodiles – the small crocodiles were real, but fortunately the largest crocodile was plastic! In the second week, the viewers decide who leaves the jungle each day. The last person left becomes King or Queen of the Jungle, and wins a lot of money for charity.

Life in the jungle isn't easy for the celebrities. They complain because they're hungry, and they often get bored because they have no contact with the outside world. They only see the show's presenters and film crews who interview them. But not too far away from the camp there are up to 400 people working on the programme!

1 Opener

Look at the photos. Which of these words do you expect to find in the text?

crocodiles   horses   insects
jungle   knives   log   market
mobile phones   rhinos
snakes   zoo

2 Presentation

🎧 Read and listen to the article *I'm A Celebrity – Get Me Out Of Here!*

80

3 Comprehension

True or false? Correct the false statements.

1. The celebrities spend up to two weeks in the jungle.
2. They must hide their cameras.
3. They can take any luxury items they want.
4. They must cook on an open fire.
5. The celebrities choose who must do the tasks to win extra food.
6. In one of the tasks, a celebrity must eat live snakes.
7. The King or Queen of the Jungle earns a lot of money.
8. The celebrities aren't always happy in the camp.

4 Grammar

Complete.

> **must and mustn't**
> The celebrities ____ give up luxuries.
> They ____ learn survival techniques.
> What kind of things ____ they do?
> They ____n't take mobile phones.
> They ____n't forget the dangers of the jungle.
>
> The past tense of *must* is *had to*.
> One person **had to** walk through water full of crocodiles.

➡ Check the answers: Grammar Summary page 114

5 Grammar Practice

Complete with *must* or *mustn't*.

1. The celebrities ____ cook their own meals.
2. They ____ go too far from the camp.
3. They ____ be careful in the jungle.
4. What ____ they do to win extra food?
5. They ____ complain too much!

6 Speaking

Read the notice and say what you must and mustn't do at the YTV studio.

> You must do what the director tells you.
> You mustn't use mobile phones.

YTV

NOTES FOR VISITORS
Read these notes carefully and enjoy your visit.

PLEASE
- Do what the director tells you.
- Stay with your group.
- Arrive and leave on time.
- Be quiet during filming.
- Clap when the 'Clap!' sign is on.

DON'T
- Use mobile phones.
- Smoke.
- Leave litter in the studio.
- Ask the actors for autographs.
- Take flash photographs.

7 Speaking

Look at the signs from the YTV studio. Ask and answer.

> Can we use a video camera?
> No, you mustn't use a video camera.

NO PHOTOGRAPHS
NO VIDEO CAMERAS
SILENCE! NO TALKING
NO ENTRY
NO EATING IN THE STUDIO
NO VISITORS IN THIS AREA
DON'T TOUCH THE EQUIPMENT

Now write a sentence for each sign.

You mustn't use a video camera.

8 Pronunciation

🎧 Listen and repeat.

/m/

You **m**ust re**m**e**m**ber **m**y **m**obile nu**m**ber – you **m**ustn't **m**ake a **m**istake.

9 Vocabulary

Match the words in box A with the words in box B to make compound words. How many of the compound words can you find in this lesson?

cooking pot

> **A**
> cooking ice film make mobile
> note snake toilet video

> **B**
> bites book camera cream crew
> phone paper pot up

10 Writing

What things must and mustn't you do in your town? Make lists of places and rules. Think about:

> on a bus   at the cinema   in a park
> at a restaurant   at school

You mustn't smoke at the cinema.
You must wait for a table at a restaurant.

Now compare your lists with other students.

7 WONDERFUL WORLD

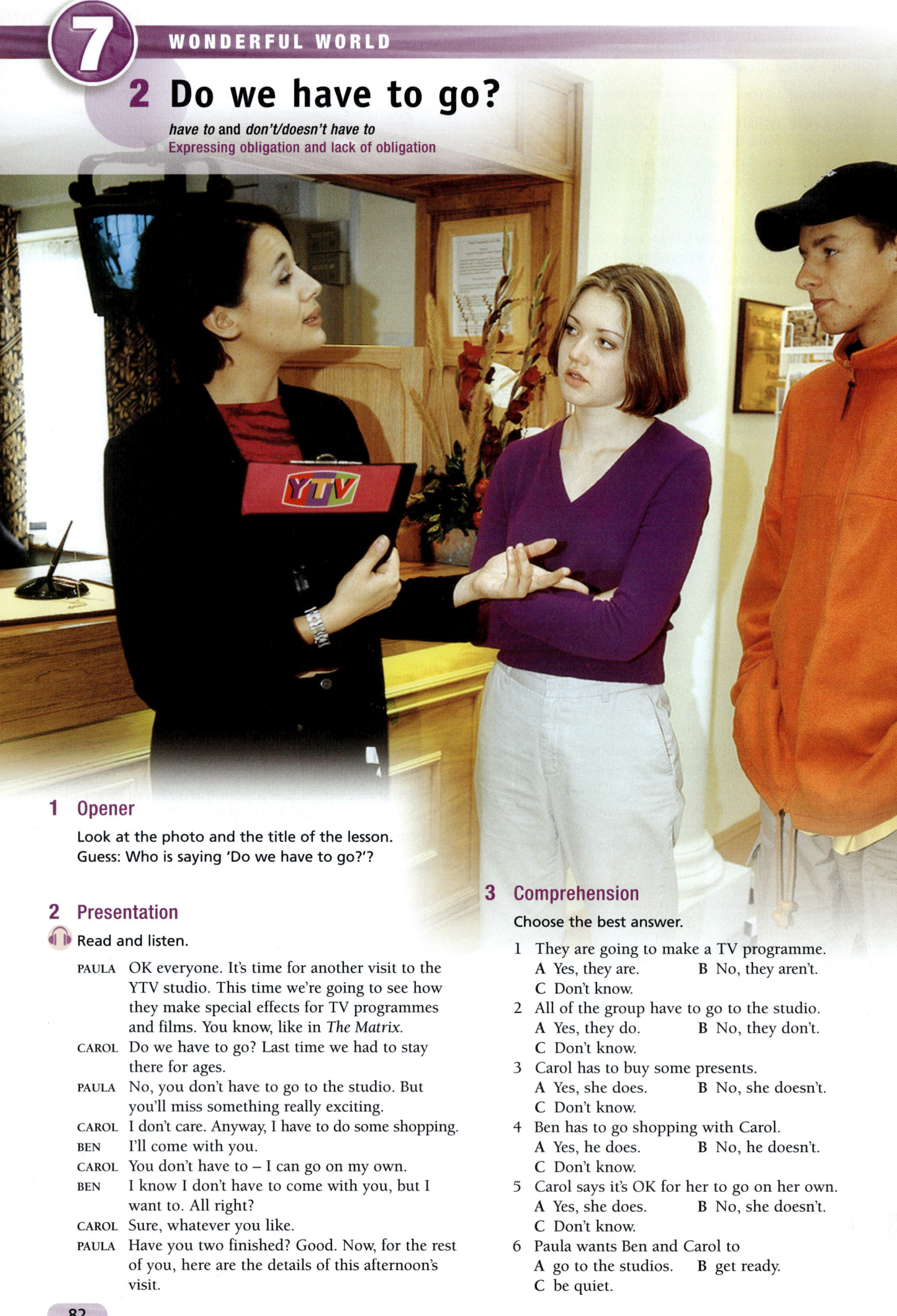

2 Do we have to go?

have to and *don't/doesn't have to*
Expressing obligation and lack of obligation

1 Opener

Look at the photo and the title of the lesson.
Guess: Who is saying 'Do we have to go?'?

2 Presentation

Read and listen.

PAULA OK everyone. It's time for another visit to the YTV studio. This time we're going to see how they make special effects for TV programmes and films. You know, like in *The Matrix*.

CAROL Do we have to go? Last time we had to stay there for ages.

PAULA No, you don't have to go to the studio. But you'll miss something really exciting.

CAROL I don't care. Anyway, I have to do some shopping.

BEN I'll come with you.

CAROL You don't have to – I can go on my own.

BEN I know I don't have to come with you, but I want to. All right?

CAROL Sure, whatever you like.

PAULA Have you two finished? Good. Now, for the rest of you, here are the details of this afternoon's visit.

3 Comprehension

Choose the best answer.

1 They are going to make a TV programme.
   A Yes, they are.   B No, they aren't.
   C Don't know.
2 All of the group have to go to the studio.
   A Yes, they do.   B No, they don't.
   C Don't know.
3 Carol has to buy some presents.
   A Yes, she does.   B No, she doesn't.
   C Don't know.
4 Ben has to go shopping with Carol.
   A Yes, he does.   B No, he doesn't.
   C Don't know.
5 Carol says it's OK for her to go on her own.
   A Yes, she does.   B No, she doesn't.
   C Don't know.
6 Paula wants Ben and Carol to
   A go to the studios.   B get ready.
   C be quiet.

4 Grammar

Complete.

> **have/has to and don't/doesn't have to**
> I _____ _____ do some shopping.
> Carol _____ _____ buy some presents.
> You _____ _____ come with me.
> Do we _____ _____ go?
>
> *have to* and *must* both express obligation.
> *don't/doesn't have to* = It's not necessary.
> *mustn't* = It's not allowed.
>
> *had to* is the past of both *have to* and *must*
> We _____ _____ stay there for ages.

➡ Check the answers: Grammar Summary page 114

5 Grammar Practice

Match the beginnings with the endings.

You have to …
1 be at the airport   a to win the competition.
2 be on time   b an hour before take-off.
3 get all the answers right c in a supermarket.
4 pass an examination   d for your lessons.
5 pay at the check-out   e when you're in a car.
6 wear a seat belt   f before you can go to university.

6 Grammar Practice

Rewrite the sentences replacing the words in italics with the correct form of *have to*.

1 The law says that you must wear a seat belt in a car.
2 *You don't need to* study every night.
3 *It's necessary to* do what the teacher says.
4 *It was necessary for me to* phone the doctor.
5 *The law says that you must* buy a ticket when you catch a train.
6 *They didn't need to* wait long for a bus.

7 Listening

🎧 Listen to Paula talking about the rules for the next YTV competition. Tick (✓) the things you have to do and cross (✗) the things you don't have to do.

1 answer three questions about New York
2 write a sentence saying why YTV is the greatest
3 pay £5 to enter the competition
4 send a photograph with your answers
5 send in your answers by 1st September
6 buy the YTV magazine
7 know New York very well
8 write clearly using a black pen
9 be over 16 to enter the competition

Now tell each other about the competition rules.

> You have to answer three questions about New York.
> > You don't have to pay £5 to enter the competition.

8 Speaking

What do you have to do every day? Write a short questionnaire. Ask about:

Meals
help with meals   lay the table   do the washing up
Clothes
wash your own clothes   do the ironing
wear school uniform
Your room
make your bed   put your clothes away
clean your room
School
walk a long way to school   catch a bus to school
do homework every night

Begin like this:

Do you have to help with meals?
Do you have to lay the table?

Ask three students the questions in your questionnaire. Compare the results.

9 Pronunciation

🎧 Listen and repeat.

/h/

How hard does a hungry horse have to work before he has some help?

10 Vocabulary

Complete the phrases with these verbs.

| catch   do   lay   make   pass |

1 _____ the table   5 _____ the bed
2 _____ the ironing   6 _____ the shopping
3 _____ a train   7 _____ a list
4 _____ an exam   8 _____ the washing up

11 Game

Say nouns which go with the verb. Use verbs from this lesson. Who can say the most nouns?

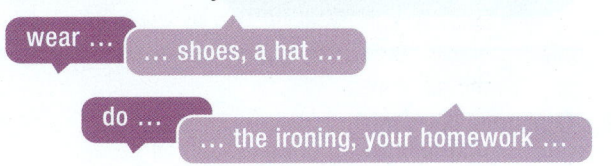

> wear …
> > … shoes, a hat …

> do …
> > … the ironing, your homework …

12 Writing

Write a paragraph about things you have to do during the week, but don't have to do at weekends.

OR Write a paragraph about things you had to and didn't have to do last weekend.

Use the questionnaire you wrote in exercise 8 to help you.

7 WONDERFUL WORLD

3 Don't be frightened!

Participial adjectives ending in *-ed/-ing*
want to/would like to   I'd rather …
Making suggestions and expressing preferences

These exhibitions are just a few highlights of …

The Natural History Museum

Fish, amphibians and reptiles
Enjoy an exhibition full of surprising fish, amphibians and reptiles, including sea creatures that live so deep they have to provide their own light, and a 150-year-old giant tortoise.

Dinosaurs
Experience the thrill and danger of life amongst the dinosaurs that lived on our planet for 160 million years! These extraordinary animals became extinct around 65 million years ago, but they come alive in our exciting animated display.

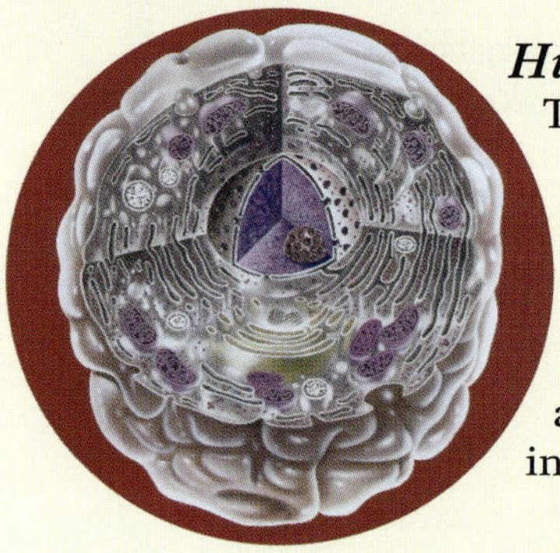

Human biology
Take a really close look at yourself – the most intelligent mammal in the world. You'll be surprised how amazing you are! Test your mind and body, and understand how they grow and develop, in this highly interactive exhibition.

The power within
Find out how shocking an earthquake feels in an earthquake simulator. Don't be frightened – it isn't real! Discover what happens when a volcano erupts and check for yourself where there have been earthquakes in the last week.

Earth today and tomorrow
This is a fascinating exhibition which shows how living things interact with each other. See how human beings are changing the environment, follow the water cycle on a huge video wall, and experience the sights and sounds of a rainforest.

---

1 Opener
Look at the photos. What can you see?

2 Presentation
Read and listen to the information about the Natural History Museum.

3 Comprehension
Answer the questions.

Which exhibition is best for someone who wants to …
1 visit the jungle?
2 understand how their brain works?
3 see an animated Tyrannosaurus Rex?
4 look at snakes?
5 find out about eruptions?

Which exhibition would you like to go to? Why?

4 Grammar

Complete with *-ed* or *-ing*.

> **Participial adjectives ending in *-ed/-ing***
> There are lots of surpris____ fish.
> You'll be surpris____ by the human body.
> Earthquakes are shock____.
> Don't be frighten____!
>
> Adjectives ending in *-ed* describe a feeling or reaction.
> Adjectives ending in *-ing* describe the **cause** of the feeling or reaction.
>
> ➡ Check the answers: Grammar Summary page 115

5 Grammar Practice

Choose the correct adjective.

1. The museum has some fascinated/fascinating exhibitions.
2. The Human biology exhibition is very interested/interesting.
3. We were amazed/amazing to see the animated dinosaurs.
4. I'm not frightened/frightening of snakes.
5. The earthquake simulator is excited/exciting.
6. They were tired/tiring after four hours in the museum.

Now write sentences using the remaining six adjectives.

We were fascinated by the Tyrannosaurus Rex.

6 Vocabulary

Match the animals with their definitions.

1 amphibians 2 birds 3 fish 4 mammals 5 reptiles

a They live in water and swim.
b They can live both in water and on land.
c They lay eggs and have short legs or no legs at all.
d They lay eggs and have two wings and feathers.
e They feed their babies with milk.

7 Listening

Carol and Ben are in the Natural History Museum. Before you listen, look at the sentences below and guess who says what.

1. I'd like to try the earthquake simulator – it sounds exciting!
2. I think earthquakes are very frightening!
3. I'd rather look at snakes.
4. I'd rather not.
5. I'd rather see the Dinosaurs exhibition.
6. I'm tired of dinosaurs.
7. What about the rainforest?
8. That sounds quite boring.
9. Would you like to go the museum café?
10. Let's go shopping!

🎧 Now listen and check.

8 Pronunciation

🎧 Listen and repeat.

> both   clothes   father   fourth   other   south
> then   think   thrill   through   together   with

Now write the words under /θ/ or /ð/ in the chart. Then listen again and check.

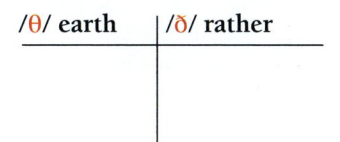

/θ/ earth	/ð/ rather

9 Role Play

Act out a conversation between two people who are trying to decide what to do or where to go. Use the phrases in the box and look back at exercise 7.

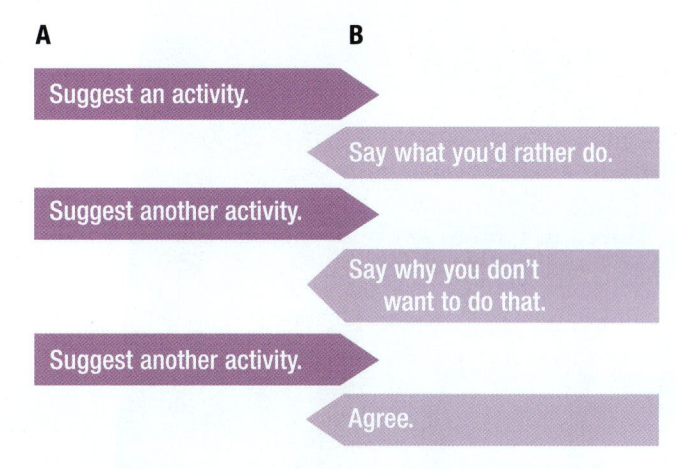

A   **B**

Suggest an activity.

　　　　　　Say what you'd rather do.

Suggest another activity.

　　　　　　Say why you don't want to do that.

Suggest another activity.

　　　　　　Agree.

> **Making suggestions and expressing preferences**
> What about …?   How about …?
> I'd like to …   I want to …
> Would you like to …?   Do you want to …?
> I'd rather …   I'd rather not.
> Let's …

10 Writing

A friend sends you this email.

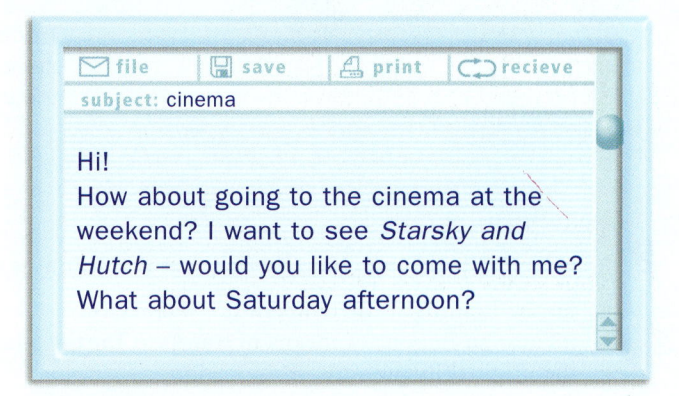

> ✉ file   💾 save   🖨 print   🔄 recieve
> **subject:** cinema
>
> Hi!
> How about going to the cinema at the weekend? I want to see *Starsky and Hutch* – would you like to come with me? What about Saturday afternoon?

You'd like to go to the cinema, but you've seen *Starsky and Hutch* and you're busy on Saturday afternoon. Write a reply suggesting another film and another time.

7 WONDERFUL WORLD

4 Integrated Skills
Describing a journey

ICE PARADISE

Lapland is a **region** north of the Arctic Circle, stretching across four countries from Russia in the east, through Finland and Sweden, to Norway in the west. Lapland is the home of the Sami people, ___1___.

Thousands of people now visit Lapland every year. A major attraction is the world-famous Ice Hotel, which is 200 kilometres inside the Arctic Circle in a small Swedish town called Jukkasjärvi.

The hotel has an ice bar, ice bedrooms, and an ice church, which is very popular for weddings. They have to rebuild the hotel in November every year ___2___ ! Most guests stay only one night in the Ice Hotel because it's **freezing**!

And now there is also the Ice Globe, a **replica** of the Globe Theatre in London! The theatre is absolutely **stunning**. You sit on ice seats covered with reindeer skins, and above the ice stage, the Northern Lights flash across the night sky. All the performances are in the Sami language. The first was Shakespeare's Hamlet, a 70-minute version because the **audience** and actors couldn't stand the cold – ___3___ !

The Ice Hotel has brought new life to the region and the increased tourism in Lapland is helping to keep the Sami **culture** alive. Jukkasjärvi has become a tourist centre; popular activities include travelling on sleds pulled by husky dogs, ___4___.

The snowmobile is not only for pleasure and fun, ___5___. **Traditionally** the Sami lived by herding reindeer, and they travelled across the ice and snow on sleds pulled by huskies or reindeer. Today they also use snowmobiles to follow the reindeer **herds** and to travel across the tundra.

1 Opener

Look at the photos. Use these words to describe what you can see.

> actors huskies ice reindeer
> sled snow stage theatre
> traditional costume

Reading

2 Read *Ice Paradise* and complete the text with phrases a–e.
  a on the first night the temperature was –31°C
  b it's also an important means of transport for the Sami people
  c the original inhabitants of the region
  d cross-country skiing and 'snowmobile safaris'
  e because it melts every spring

🎧 Now listen and check.

What do you think is the most surprising information in the text?

3 Find the **highlighted** words in the text which mean:
  1 people watching a play *n*
  2 area *n*
  3 way of life *n*
  4 exact copy *n*
  5 the way people have usually done something *adv*
  6 extremely cold *adj*
  7 groups of animals *n*
  8 amazing *adj*

86

Listening

4 An English woman, Gill Brown, travelled to the Arctic for charity. Read the beginning of her story and questions 1–8. Then listen and choose the correct answers.

I like the cold, I don't like hot places, and I'm interested in dogs, I love dogs, so when I saw an advertisement for an eight-day trip to the Arctic running a team of husky dogs, I thought – this is just too good to miss! I have to do it! But I was worried because I'm very frightened of flying, and I had to fly for the first time in 15 years!

1. How much money did Gill raise for charity?
   A £500   B £5000
2. When did she fly to Sweden?
   A 13th March   B 30th March
3. Why was the flight to Sweden frightening?
   A It was very windy.   B It was very cold.
4. How far did the group have to travel with the dogs?
   A 40 kms   B 400 kms
5. How many people were there in the group?
   A 14   B 40
6. How many dogs were there in each team?
   A 60   B 4
7. How did Gill feel when she fell off her sled?
   A Embarrassed.   B Embarrassing.
8. How did she feel at the end of each day?
   A Exhausted.   B Exhausting.

5 Listen to the next part of Gill's story.

Student A

Listen and note down the answers to these questions.

1. Did they stay in different places every night?
2. What time did they get up every morning?
3. How many hours did they travel every day?
4. What was the worst part of the trip?
5. What was one of the best things about the trip?

Student B

Listen and note down the answers to these questions.

1. What did Gill do every evening?
2. What time did they leave in the mornings?
3. When did they stay at the Ice Hotel?
4. Where did Gill see a wonderful Sami performance?
5. Does Gill want to go back to the Arctic?

6 Speaking

Students A and B work together. Use your notes from exercise 5 to tell each other about the trip.

7 Writing

Imagine that you were with the group that went to the Arctic. Write a paragraph describing your trip.

OR Write a paragraph about a different trip – real or imaginary!

- Where did you go?
- How long was the trip?
- How did you get there?
- What did you do?
- What was the best/worst thing about the trip?

Learner Independence

8 It's good to try out lots of ways of learning. What is the easiest way for you to learn new words? Order these ways 1–7.

- Using new words in speaking activities.
- Drawing pictures of the new word.
- Looking at the parts of a word.
- Playing games and doing crosswords.
- Writing sentences using the new words.
- Putting words in groups and making word maps.
- Associating the word with something else.

Now compare with another student. Try another way of learning words.

9 Read this list of ways to improve your English.

> I must try to guess the meaning of new words before I look them up.
> I mustn't be embarrassed about making mistakes when I speak English.
> I must learn ten new words everyday.
> I must read a graded reader a week.
> I must ask the teacher for help more often.
> I mustn't forget to take my dictionary to class.
> I must keep a vocabulary notebook.

Choose three ways and compare your choices with other students. Try out your choices.

10 Phrasebook

Listen and repeat these useful expressions.

> I don't care.   I'd like to try it.   It sounds exciting.
> No way!   I'd rather not.   That sounds quite boring.
> Would you like to … ?   It's freezing.
> I like the cold.   It's too good to miss!

Would *you* like to go to the Arctic? Say why or why not. Use some of the expressions in the box.

Unit 7 Communication Activity
Student **A** page 108
Student **B** page 118

7 WONDERFUL WORLD
Inspiration *Extra!*

PROJECT Extreme Places File

Make a file about extreme places.

1. Work in a group and look at Unit 7 again. Note down words that describe weather and geographical features. Make a list of other extreme places – places which are very hot, cold, wet or dry. Then choose one or two to write about.

2. Find out information about each place:

   > Where is it?   Who lives there?
   > What kind of wildlife is there?
   > What is the landscape like? (Jungle, desert, or ice and snow? Are there hills, rivers, lakes, trees?)
   > What is the weather like?
   > Maximum and minimum temperatures?

3. Work together and make an Extreme Places File. Read it carefully and correct any mistakes. Draw pictures or find photographs from magazines or newspapers for your file. Show your Extreme Places File to the other groups.

GAME Desert Island

- Work in groups of three or four.
- You are going to spend six months on a desert island. Each group can only take five things with them, apart from food and clothing. Discuss with your group what you would like to take, and agree on a list of five items.
- Each group explains their choice of items to the class.
- The class votes on the best list.

LIMERICK

Read and listen.

A dinosaur walked into town.
He found a huge chair and sat down.
'Now why did you think
that I was extinct?'
the dinosaur roared with a frown.

SKETCH Rooms

Read and listen.

BOY We must find somewhere to stay soon – I'm exhausted.
GIRL Let's try this hotel – the sign says *Rooms*!
They go into the building.
MAN Good evening – can I help you?
GIRL Yes, we'd like two rooms, please.
MAN What kind of rooms would you like?
BOY What kind of rooms?
MAN Yes – kitchens, sitting rooms, dining rooms …?
BOY Er – we'd like two bedrooms!
GIRL With bathrooms.
MAN Two bedrooms *and* two bathrooms?
GIRL Yes, and we'd like to have breakfast.
MAN Breakfast?! But it's six o'clock in the evening!
BOY We don't want to have breakfast now!
MAN We don't serve breakfast at any time!
GIRL Oh! But –
MAN Don't you want to see the rooms? Don't you want to know the prices?
BOY How much do they cost?
MAN Two bedrooms and two bathrooms? Oh, about £5,000.
GIRL £5,000 – for one night! Without breakfast!
BOY That's absurd! We can't stay here!
MAN No one has ever wanted to stay here before.
GIRL I'm not surprised! This hotel is extremely expensive!
MAN But this isn't a hotel!
BOY Isn't it?
MAN No, this is an office – we sell room designs!

Now act out the sketch in groups of three.

REVISION for more practice

LESSON 1

Write sentences about things you must and mustn't do in these places:

> at a swimming pool   at the theatre   in a library

You must have a shower before you swim.

Look at page 81, exercises 6 and 7, for ideas.

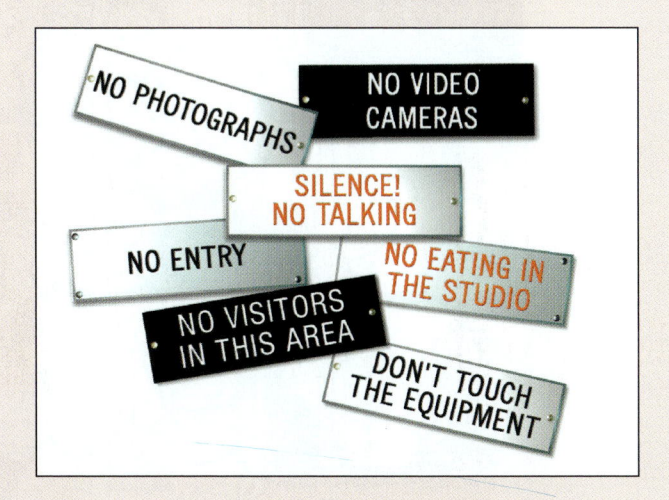

LESSON 2

Look at page 83, exercise 7. Write ten sentences about the rules for the next YTV competition using *have to* and *don't have to*.

You have to answer three questions about New York.

LESSON 3

Look at the text on page 84. Choose the two most interesting exhibitions and write sentences saying why you would like to go to them.

LESSON 4

Write a list of as many animals as possible. Put the animals into groups: amphibians, birds, fish, mammals, reptiles.

EXTENSION for language development

LESSON 1

Write a list of things people must and mustn't do in extreme places.

People in very hot places must drink lots of water ...

LESSON 2

Imagine that you are flying to London tomorrow. Write sentences about what you have to do before you go.

I have to pack my suitcase.

LESSON 3

Write five sentences saying what you would like/want to do in the next five years. Then exchange sentences with another student. Write responses to your partner's sentences using *I'd rather ... .*

I'd like to visit the USA.
I'd rather go to Brazil.

I want to get a job.
I'd rather go to university.

LESSON 4

Look at pages 86–87 and write sentences about the lesson topics using at least six of these words.

> amazed   amazing   excited   exciting   fascinated
> fascinating   frightened   frightening   interested
> interesting   surprised   surprising   tired   tiring

The Ice Globe theatre sounds amazing and I'd love to see a performance there.

UNIT 7

89

culture

Do the right thing! ✓

QUIZ

Here is some information for visitors to Britain. But half of the statements are false! Can you find the five true statements?

In Britain ...   True False

1 You must cycle and drive on the left-hand side of the road.   ☐   ☐
2 When you're waiting for a bus, you don't have to queue.   ☐   ☐
3 Everyone has eggs and bacon for breakfast.   ☐   ☐
4 When you've finished eating, you should put your knife and fork together in the centre of the plate. ☐   ☐
5 Most people drink tea with milk.   ☐   ☐
6 When someone invites you to a party, you must arrive five minutes early. ☐   ☐
7 When you visit someone's home, you have to take off your shoes. ☐   ☐
8 Lots of shops are open seven days a week.   ☐   ☐
9 Girls and boys mustn't kiss on their first date.   ☐   ☐
10 People can get married when they are 16.   ☐   ☐

🎧 Now listen and check.

1 Comprehension

Match the beginnings with the endings to make *true* sentences about life in Britain.

1 You mustn't
2 You should always stand
3 Many people don't have anything
4 You put your knife and fork together
5 A few people drink
6 It's not polite
7 You don't take off your shoes
8 Lots of people
9 Young people don't
10 People can't

a to show you don't want any more to eat.
b go shopping on Sundays.
c to arrive early for a party.
d get married until they're 16.
e in the queue for a bus.
f have to kiss on their first date.
g drive on the right.
h when you visit people.
i tea without milk.
j to eat for breakfast.

2 Writing

Write some (true!) information for visitors to your country. Think about:

cycling and driving   queueing   typical food and drink
mealtimes and table manners   visiting people
shopping hours   dating and marriage

Use the ideas on this page to help you.

culture

Saying it without words

We use words to communicate with people, but we also use body language – particularly gestures and facial expressions. And different people have different body language …

1 _____

Older people in Britain usually shake hands when they meet for the first time, but young people don't do this very often. In France, many people of all ages shake hands every time they see each other – they say the French spend 20 minutes a day shaking hands! In Britain, men often kiss women friends once or twice on the cheek and women sometimes kiss each other too, but men don't usually kiss each other. However, Russian men often kiss each other, and men in the Arab world often hug and kiss each other on the cheek. Meanwhile, in Japan, people bow when they meet each other; neither men nor women kiss in public.

2 _____

Americans like people who smile and agree with them, but Australians are more interested in people who disagree with them. So sometimes Americans think Australians are rude and unfriendly, and Australians think polite, friendly Americans are boring! In Europe, it's friendly to smile at strangers, but in many Asian countries it isn't polite. And in Japan you must cover your mouth when you smile or laugh.

3 _____

In Western cultures, young people and adults look each other in the eye during a conversation to show interest and trust, but in many Asian countries, it's rude to look people in the eye, especially a superior such as a teacher. In Britain and the United States it isn't polite to stare at strangers, but Indians often look long and thoughtfully at people they don't know.

4 _____

In Britain, it's polite to respond during conversations and to make comments to show that you're interested. But in parts of Northern Europe and in Japan, it's quite common for people to stay silent when someone is talking to them. In China, Japan, and Korea, young people don't usually start conversations with adults and only speak if an adult speaks to them. In contrast, Americans encourage young people to start conversations.

3 Reading

Read *Saying it without words* and match these headings with paragraphs 1–4.

Silence   Eye contact
Greetings   Facial expression

🎧 Now listen and check.

4 Vocabulary

Match these words with their definitions.

1 facial *adj*
2 hug *v*
3 bow *v*
4 rude *adj*
5 superior *n*
6 stare *v*
7 respond *v*
8 common *adj*

a not polite
b look for a long time
c usual
d of the face
e reply
f bend your body forward
g put your arms round
h someone in a higher position

Which sentences in the text describe what is happening in the photos?

5 Comprehension

Answer the questions.

In which country or countries do …
1 people shake hands a lot?
2 people not look superiors in the eye?
3 young people wait for adults to talk to them?
4 people sometimes not respond during conversations?
5 men put their arms round each other?
6 people put their hand over their mouth when they laugh?

6 Writing

How do you say things without words? For each of the four topics in the text, write sentences about how people in your country behave.

91

8 MOVING IMAGES

1 The characters seem to speak

Infinitive of purpose
Verb + infinitive
Connector: *so*
Describing a process
Expressing purpose and consequence

The *Wallace and Gromit* Story

People all over the world know the *Wallace and Gromit* short animated films. Animated simply means that they use models to make the films, not actors. The *Wallace and Gromit* story started over 30 years ago when two schoolboys, David Sproxton and Peter Lord, learnt to make animated films using David's father's 16mm camera. The BBC offered to buy one of their first films and in 1972 David and Peter started their studio, Aardman Animations. They decided to call it Aardman (it sounds like 'hard man') after the name of a character in their first film.

In 1985 Nick Park joined the studio to work on a film about a cheese-loving inventor, Wallace, and his dog, Gromit, called *A Grand Day Out* (1989). Two more films, *The Wrong Trousers* (1993) and *A Close Shave* (1995) followed.

How do they make animated films?
First the animator draws a 'storyboard', a series of pictures of the film. The animator uses the storyboard to plan the film in detail.

Then they make a model of the character and the designer plans the background. The models are often quite small, smaller than the human hand. Next the director has a rehearsal to make sure that everyone knows what they are doing. After that, they are ready to shoot the film. They record the voices and the animator moves the models' mouths, so the characters seem to speak.

In one minute of film each character can move up to 1,440 times! The film-makers often only manage to shoot three seconds of film a day, so it can take years to make a whole animated film.

1 Opener

Look at the photos. Have you seen a *Wallace and Gromit* film? What other animated films do you know?

2 Presentation

Read and listen to the article about *Wallace and Gromit*.

3 Comprehension

Answer the questions.

1 What equipment did David and Peter use to make their first animated films?
2 Why did they decide to call their studio Aardman?
3 Why did Nick Park join Aardman?
4 What is a storyboard?
5 Why does the director have a rehearsal?
6 Why do the characters seem to speak?
7 Which information shows that making an animated film is a very slow process?

4 Grammar

Complete.

> **Infinitive of purpose**
> They use models **to make** the films.
> Nick Park joined the studio ____ ____ on a film.
> The animator uses the storyboard ____ ____ the film.
>
> We use the infinitive of purpose to say ____ we do something.

> **Verb + infinitive**
> The BBC offered **to buy** one of their first films.
> They decided ____ ____ it Aardman.
> They often only manage ____ ____ three seconds of film.

➡ Check the answers: Grammar Summary page 115

5 Grammar Practice

Match the words in list A with the phrases in list B and write sentences beginning *You use a ... to ...*

A	B
camera	send email
computer	take photographs
lifebelt	listen to music
map	save someone in the water
microphone	carry things on your back
mobile	find the way
rucksack	make a recording
Walkman	send a text message

6 Game

Play *What is it?*

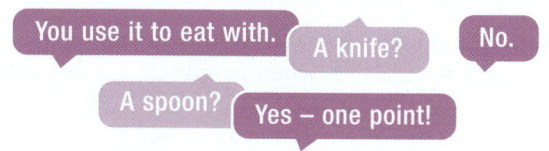

- You use it to eat with.
- A knife?
- No.
- A spoon?
- Yes – one point!

7 Pronunciation

Mark the stressed syllable.

> animated   animation   background   character
> designer   detail   inventor   manage   storyboard

🎧 Now listen and check. Repeat the words.

8 Listening

🎧 Carol, Ben and Jack are at the YTV goodbye party. Listen and match the beginnings with the endings.

1 Ben wanted   a to get Carol a drink.
2 Carol refused   b not to tell Ben.
3 Jack offered   c to dance with Ben.
4 Carol agreed   d to stop arguing.
5 Jack promised   e to dance with Carol.
6 Carol told Jack and Ben   f to write to Jack.

Now ask and answer.

- What did Ben want?
- He wanted to dance with Carol.

9 Role Play

Act out a conversation at a party between two friends at the end of a holiday.

A | B

- Invite B to dance.
- Refuse and give a reason.
- Offer to get B a drink.
- Thank A but ask for something else.
- Say how you feel about the end of the holiday.
- Agree. Ask A to promise to do something.
- Promise. Invite B to visit you.
- Accept.

10 Vocabulary

Look at the personal information and match the people with the jobs in the box. Then say what each person wants to be.

> Ben likes flying, so he wants to be a pilot.

- Ben likes flying.
- Gabi is good at languages.
- Jack likes mathematics.
- Sally is good at science and likes helping people.
- Laura likes writing and taking photographs.
- Pedro likes making videos.
- Tomek enjoys playing the guitar.
- Carol loves going to the theatre.

> **Jobs and occupations**
> actor   computer expert   doctor   journalist
> musician   pilot   tourist guide   TV producer

> **Connector *so***
> The animator moves the models, **so** the characters seem to speak.
>
> We use *so* to talk about consequence or result.

11 Writing

Think about what people in your class like or are good at. Write sentences saying what you think they would like to be.

Karl loves blowing whistles, so I think he'd like to be a referee.

8 MOVING IMAGES

2 If you like a boy …

Open conditional with *if/when*
Talking about cause and effect
Describing how things work

1 Opener

Who is in the photo? What do fortune tellers do?

2 Presentation

🎧 Read and listen.

There's a surprise guest at the YTV goodbye party. It's Mona, the YTV fortune teller.

MONA Give me your hand, Carol, because I can read your character by looking at the lines on it. Now, is there anything you want to ask me?

CAROL This sounds silly, I know, but there are two boys here tonight. I really like both of them. And they both want to see me again after the holiday. But I don't know what to say.

MONA Mmm. Let me see. Yes, it's hard for you to show your feelings.

CAROL To tell the truth, I've been rude to both of them. I didn't mean to be, but …

MONA If you like a boy, you're rude because you want to hide your feelings. Perhaps you're nervous.

CAROL I'm not usually nervous when I meet people. But I don't like it when people tell me what to do.

MONA And what do you do if people are bossy?

CAROL I lose my temper. I've shouted at Greg …

MONA How do you feel when you're on your own?

CAROL That's a good question. When I'm on my own, I get depressed, you know, really down.

MONA So why can't you see both boys after the holiday?

CAROL Because they say I must choose one of them!

3 Comprehension

Complete these sentences about Carol.

1 She _____ know what to say to Ben and Jack.
2 She _____ _____ it when people _____ her what to do.
3 She _____ usually nervous when she _____ people.
4 She _____ her temper if people are bossy.
5 If _____ on her own, she _____ depressed.
6 She can't see both boys after the holiday because they say she _____ _____ one of them.

4 Grammar

Complete.

Open conditional with *if/when*
If you **like** a boy, you**'re** rude.
When I'm on my own, I _____ depressed.
I _____ _____ it when people tell me what to do.
What _____ you do if people are bossy?
How _____ you _____ when you're on your own?

In open conditional sentences, both verbs are in the _____ _____ tense.

➡ Check the answers: Grammar Summary page 115

94

5 Grammar Practice

Read *How a Digital Camera Works* and match the beginnings with the endings.

1 Both digital and traditional cameras take pictures
2 When you take a picture with a digital camera,
3 A digital camera uses numbers
4 When you look at digital photos,
5 You get white light
6 The computer makes millions of calculations

a if you mix red, green and blue.
b when it records what it sees.
c they are in colour.
d when you press the button.
e when it compares what each pixel 'sees'.
f each pixel records the brightness of the light.

6 Vocabulary

Match the words with their definitions.

1 compare   2 digital   3 make calculations
4 pixel   5 primary colours   6 traditional

a of the usual kind, not modern
b square on a computer chip which measures light
c recording information as numbers
d you mix them to make other colours
e see how things are the same or different
f use mathematics to work out answers

7 Pronunciation

Listen and repeat. Which word does not end in the sound /əl/?

> angel   animal   digital   football   inflammable
> local   model   musical   noodle   original   pixel
> rehearsal   squirrel   terrible   travel   whistle

8 Speaking

Complete these statements about another student without talking to him/her. Then compare your statements.

Your favourite song is 'If I'm not the one you want, I'll be the one you need' by NSYNC.

> **This is You**
> ★ Your favourite song is …
> ★ You are very happy when you …
> ★ You don't like it when people …
> ★ If you get into trouble, you …
> ★ Your favourite food is …
> ★ When you meet someone new, you feel …
> ★ If you get angry, you …
> ★ You feel good if you …
> ★ Your favourite colour is …

9 Writing

Complete the statements in exercise 8 about yourself and add five more.

HOW A DIGITAL CAMERA WORKS

Digital cameras and traditional cameras do the same thing: they take pictures when you press the button. But the way they take pictures is quite different.

For a start, digital cameras don't use a film. Instead they have a computer chip covered in millions of tiny squares. These squares are called pixels and they measure the light. When you press the button on a digital camera, each pixel records the brightness of the light it 'sees'. When the camera records what it sees, it uses numbers not images.

Now here's a surprise! The pixels only record light and dark. So do digital cameras only take black and white pictures? No, when you look at digital photos, they are in colour. So where does the colour come from?

There are three *primary* colours of light: red, green and blue. When we mix red, green and blue light, we get white. If we mix red and green, we get yellow, and so on. This is how your eyes, a computer screen and a digital camera work. In a digital camera there is a filter in front of each pixel, so it 'sees' only one of the three colours.

There's a computer in your digital camera which mixes the colours. When you take a picture, the computer compares what each pixel 'sees' with the other pixels around it. During this process, the computer makes millions of calculations in a few seconds.

8 MOVING IMAGES

3 You're brilliant, aren't you?

Question tags with *be*
Asking for agreement

1 Opener

Look at the pictures in the YTV London Quiz and tell each other what they show.

LONDON QUIZ YTV

How much do you know about London? Find out here!

1. Where do you see lots of pigeons?
   A In Covent Garden. B In Hyde Park. C In Trafalgar Square.

2. In photo A, someone is having a great time at a carnival. Where?
   A In Covent Garden. B In Hyde Park. C In Notting Hill.

3. What are the people in photo B celebrating?
   A New Year's Eve B Chinese New Year C Christmas

4. How long did the Great Fire of London burn?
   A For four days. B For a week. C For ten days.

5. What's unusual about the roof of the Globe Theatre?
   A It's 400 years old. B It's thatched. C Christopher Wren designed it.

6. What's special about the London Eye?
   A It's the highest wheel in Europe.
   B It's the longest bridge in the world.
   C It's the tallest monument in the world.

7. Where can you take a cruise?
   A In the London Aquarium. B At Buckingham Palace. C On the Thames.

8. There's a very popular soap about London. What's it called?
   A *EastEnders* B *Emmerdale* C *Neighbours*

9. Where is the Science Museum?
   A In Oxford Street. B In South Kensington. C In Regent's Park.

10. What's the name of the famous department store in Knightsbridge?
    A Selfridges B Madame Tussaud's C Harrods

11. When did the London underground open?
    A 1863 B 1890 C 1999

12. The Natural History Museum has a simulator – what does it simulate?
    A An underground train. B An earthquake. C A TV studio.

2 Presentation

Read the conversation and do the quiz.

🎧 Now listen and check your answers.

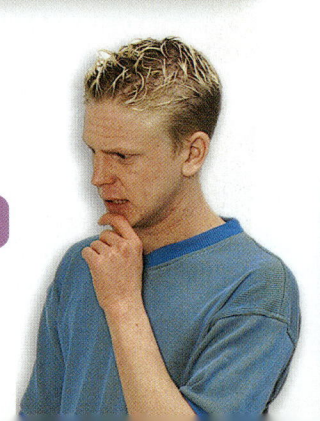

> Greg, you're an expert on London, aren't you?
>
> Well, it's my job, isn't it?
>
> So do you want to try the YTV London Quiz?
>
> I'll have a go!

3 Grammar

Complete.

Question tags

It's my job, **isn't it?**

You're an expert on London, _____n't you?

They're celebrating Chinese New Year, _____n't they?

It was a long time, **wasn't it?**

The questions were quite easy, _____n't they?

➡ Check the answers: Grammar Summary page 115

4 Grammar Practice

Complete with these question tags.

isn't he?   isn't she?   aren't they?   wasn't it?
wasn't she?   weren't they?

1 Carol and Jack are English, _____
2 Kate is a YTV producer, _____
3 Pedro is packing his suitcase, _____
4 The group were at the Notting Hill carnival, _____
5 Gabi was on the boat, _____
6 It was a great holiday, _____

5 Pronunciation

🎧 Listen and check your answers to exercise 4. Repeat the sentences.

6 Speaking

Say three things about each photo using question tags. Say:

- who's in the photo
- where they were
- what they were doing

Photo A

> Greg is in the photo, isn't he?

> They were in Covent Garden, weren't they?

> They were listening to the busker, weren't they?

7 Listening

🎧 It is the end of the party. What do you think Carol will say to Ben and Jack? Listen and find out.

Who are Ben, Carol and Jack with at the end of the party?

8 Writing

Write a short description of a place in London.

Now read out your description but don't say the name. Can the other students guess?

> It's near Regent's Park and it's full of models of famous people.

> It's Madame Tussaud's, isn't it?

UNIT 8

97

8 MOVING IMAGES

4 Integrated Skills
Describing a process

WALKING WITH DINOSAURS

You can see models of dinosaurs in London's Natural History Museum and some of the models move and roar! But a recent BBC TV series called *Walking With Dinosaurs* really brings them to life.

In *Walking With Dinosaurs* we see these huge animals eating, running and fighting on our TV screens. But the last dinosaur died 65 million years ago. So how did the BBC make the seven-part series? How can you film an animal which doesn't exist?

'It wasn't easy,' says Tim Haines, the producer of the series. 'First we spent two years talking to scientists, and reading everything about the dinosaurs. It's important to remember that dinosaurs lived in a world as real as ours – there was a sun and a moon, day, night, rain, wind, and food like today.

Next we chose dinosaurs which people knew a lot about. It's lucky that there are so many dinosaur bones around the world.

Then we found places which look like the world 65 to 230 million years ago. We went all over the world – to Chile and to New Zealand, for example. The dinosaurs are not real, but the trees, the sky, the ground, the rivers and sea all are. One problem was that when dinosaurs lived there was no grass, so we looked for places without grass.

After that, we filmed the places with people instead of dinosaurs! The film crew moved things, splashed water, broke trees and so on, in front of the camera just like a dinosaur.

Finally, back in the studio, we used computers to take the people out of the pictures, and put the dinosaurs in.'

The films are amazing – you really feel that you are watching live dinosaurs. So how did Tim Haines' team make the dinosaurs?

UNIT 8

1 **Opener**

When did the last dinosaur die? 65 million, 100 million or 230 million years ago?

2 **Reading**

🎧 Read *Walking With Dinosaurs* and number the sentences to show the order in which Tim's team did things.

- A They filmed using people not dinosaurs.
- B They decided which dinosaurs to film.
- C They found out as much as possible about the animals.
- D Computers put dinosaurs in the film instead of people.
- E They looked for places like those where the dinosaurs lived.

3 **Listening**

🎧 How did Tim's team make the dinosaurs? Listen to an interview with Tim and number A–E to show the right order.

- A Use the computer to make the animal move.
- B Scan the model into the computer.
- C Put the animal into the film picture.
- D Colour the animal's skin.
- E Make a white model of the animal.

4 **Speaking**

Look at the pictures at the bottom of page 98. Tell each other how to make a computer animation of an animal.

> First you make a white model of the animal …

5 **Writing**

Complete this process description of how they made the dinosaurs.

> 'It's called computer animation – we used models and computers. First we __1__. Next we __2__. Then we __3__. After that, __4__. Finally __5__.'

Learner Independence

6 If people don't understand you, it's important to be able to explain what you mean. Defining words is a good way to practise this skill. Find the words to complete these definitions.

1 The _____ is in charge of the film.
2 The film _____ is the group of people who help make the film.
3 A _____ is a place where you can learn about history.
4 People use computer _____ to make models move like real animals.
5 A _____ is a number of TV programmes about the same thing.

7 Write definitions of these people and things. Then check your definitions in the dictionary.

> animated films   digital camera   fortune teller
> inventor   rehearsal   storyboard   text message

Now read out your definitions but don't say the word. Can the other students guess?

8 This is the last unit of the book. What can you do to practise English in the holidays? Which of these resources can you use?

> the Internet   friends   this book   video camera
> video or DVD player   graded readers
> TV and radio   CD player   yourself

Match the resources with these activities.

1 Talk to yourself in English (silently!) when you are walking somewhere.
2 Watch or listen to English language programmes.
3 Film yourself talking in English and then watch it.
4 Use email to contact other learners of English.
5 Listen to songs in English and read the words.
6 Watch recordings of films in English.
7 Read lots of books in English.
8 Look back through it and revise what you have learnt.
9 Phone a friend every day for five minutes' conversation in English.

Choose resources and activities which you can use in the holidays.

9 **Phrasebook**

🎧 Listen and repeat these useful expressions.

Then find them in this unit.

> This sounds silly I know, but …
> But I don't know what to say.
> Let me see.
> To tell the truth, …
> That's a good question.
> I get depressed, you know, really down.
> I'll have a go.
> It wasn't easy.

Complete these two sentences for yourself.

This sounds silly, I know, but …
To tell the truth, …

Now exchange sentences with another student. Write responses to your partner's sentences.

Unit 8 Communication Activity
Student **A** page 108
Student **B** page 118

8 MOVING IMAGES

Inspiration Extra!

PROJECT London Top Ten File

Make a file about the top ten places to visit in London.

1. Work in a group and look back through *Inspiration 2*. Find the descriptions and photos of places in London. Make a list of all the places and then choose your top ten places to visit.

2. Find out information about the places from *Inspiration 2,* guidebooks and the Internet.

> What's the place called?   Where is it?
> When is it open?   How much does it cost?
> What's special about it?

3. Work together and make a London Top Ten File. Read it carefully and correct any mistakes. Copy pictures from *Inspiration 2* or find photographs from magazines or newspapers for your file. Show your London Top Ten File to the other groups.

GAME Compliments

- Think about someone you like a lot, perhaps a friend or a member of your family. Note down words to describe the person. Compare your words with other students and write them on the board.

  amazing, easy to talk to, exciting, fantastic, fascinating, friendly, interesting ...

- Use the words on the board to write a sentence about another student (don't use their name!) and give it to your teacher.

  She is friendly and warm. She helped me a lot with English.

- Now listen as your teacher reads out the sentences. Guess who they are about and who wrote them.

SONG

Read and complete with these words. One word is used twice.

> boys   father   fun   home   one
> phone   right   sun   world

Girls Just Want To Have Fun
Cyndi Lauper

I come _____ in the morning light
My mother says when you gonna live your life _____
Oh mama dear we're not the fortunate ones
And girls they want to have fun
Oh girls just want to have fun

The _____ rings in the middle of the night
My _____ yells what you gonna do with your life
Oh daddy dear you know you're still number _____
But girls they want to have fun
Oh girls just want to have

That's all they really want
Some _____
When the working day is done
Oh girls – they want to have fun
Oh girls just want to have fun

Some _____ take a beautiful girl
And hide her away from the rest of the _____
I want to be the one to walk in the _____
Oh girls – they want to have fun
Oh girls just want to have

That's all they really want
Some _____
When the working day is done
Oh girls – they want to have fun
Oh girls just want to have fun
They just want to, they just want to
They just want to, they just want to
Oh girls, girls just want to have fun ...

🎧 Now listen and check.

UNIT 8

REVISION *for more practice*

LESSON 1

Look at exercise 8 on page 93. Make questions from sentence beginnings 1–6 using 'What … ?' and answer them.

1 Ben wanted …

What did Ben want to do?
He wanted to dance with Carol.

LESSON 2

Write five sentences beginning 'When I …' using the phrases in the box, and complete them for yourself.

get hungry   feel tired   feel thirsty
am bored   am on my own

When I get hungry, I have something to eat.

LESSON 3

Write five sentences about the characters in *Inspiration 2* beginning '… is/are …' and ending in a question tag.

Pedro is from Rio, isn't he?

LESSON 4

Put the sentences in the right order. Then complete them with *First … Next … Then … After that, … Finally …*.

How to record a TV programme
A _____ watch the programme after you have recorded it.
B _____ find a new video cassette.
C _____ set the time and channel on the video recorder and press 'Record'.
D _____ decide which programme to record.
E _____ put the cassette in the video recorder.

EXTENSION *for language development*

LESSON 1

Read *The Wallace and Gromit Story* on page 92 again. Then close the book and write a description of how they make animated films using these key words:

storyboard   model   rehearsal   shoot   record
mouths   1,440 times   3 seconds

LESSON 2

Read the conversation between Carol and the fortune teller on page 94 again. Imagine you visit the fortune teller. Write a dialogue between you and the fortune teller.

LESSON 3

Look at the YTV London Quiz on page 96, and prepare another 12-question quiz about *Inspiration 2*. You can ask any questions you like but don't repeat the questions on page 96. Write the answers. Then ask another student to do your quiz.

LESSON 4

Write a paragraph about what you do every morning from the moment you wake up until you leave for school.

First I turn off the alarm clock …

101

REVIEW UNITS 7-8

Grammar

1 Read and complete. For each number 1–10, choose word A, B or C.

TOP AIR TRAVEL TIPS

Safety and security are the top priority for all airlines, and flying is the safest way to travel. Each year the world's air travellers make 1.5 billion journeys and on average there are only 50 fatal accidents. But there are lots of things which you can do __1__ your journey safer and more enjoyable.

Pack your suitcase or rucksack yourself and never offer __2__ a packet for someone else.

Make sure you check in early. Most airlines say you __3__ to check in at least one hour before a short flight and two hours before intercontinental flights. However, security checks and baggage X-rays can __4__ a long time and you don't want __5__ your flight, so allow an extra half-hour.

Remember that you __6__ have sharp things like scissors or knives in your hand baggage.

On the plane you __7__ stay in your seat all the time. It's good to walk around and stretch your legs.

You __8__ wear a seat belt for take-off and landing, but it's a good idea to keep it on all the time you are in your seat.

You __9__ listen carefully to the safety instructions so that if there __10__ an accident, you know how to get out of the plane quickly.

1	A make	B making	C to make
2	A take	B taking	C to take
3	A have	B must	C can
4	A be	B take	C make
5	A miss	B to miss	C missing
6	A don't have to	B can't have to	C mustn't
7	A have to	B don't have to	C mustn't
8	A must	B have	C can
9	A don't have to	B can	C must
10	A be	B is	C was

2 Choose *must* or *mustn't*.

YTV Competition Rules

You (1) must/mustn't be over 12 and under 21. Competitors under 16 (2) must/mustn't have their parents' permission. You (3) must/mustn't cheat and you (4) must/mustn't send in more than one entry. You (5) must/mustn't sign your entry form yourself. You (6) must/mustn't send your entry to YTV in London and it (7) must/mustn't arrive after 1 August. Winners (8) must/mustn't be ready to travel to London in August.

3 Make true sentences.

You have to	buy a ticket take exercise see a dentist have lights look left and right wear trainers be polite speak English	when/if you	want to keep fit. cross a road. cycle at night. talk to teachers. visit London. go to the cinema. have toothache. do aerobics.

4 Kate's sister, Jenny, is on a painting course in France. Ask and answer questions beginning *Does she have to …?*

speak French ✓

— Does she have to speak French?
— Yes, she does.

1 paint for four hours a day ✓
2 telephone home every day ✗
3 read a lot of books ✗
4 go to all the classes ✓
5 eat French food ✓
6 share a room ✗

5 Choose the correct adjective.

1 Gill is very interested/interesting in dogs.
2 Her flight from London to Sweden was very frightened/frightening.
3 Her first day on the sled was terrified/terrifying.
4 She was really embarrassed/embarrassing when she fell off the sled.
5 She found the whole trip absolutely exhausted/exhausting.
6 The Northern Lights were amazed/amazing.
7 Gill was surprised/surprising how much she enjoyed the trip.

6 Complete with *I'd like* or *I'd rather*.

1 Ben: '_____ to try the earthquake simulator.'
2 Carol: '_____ go shopping.'
3 Ben: '_____ not look at the snakes.'
4 Ben: '_____ to go to the museum café.'
5 Carol: '_____ go to the museum shop.'

7 Make sentences.

Tomek was very busy on his last day in London. Match the places in the box with the phrases to make sentences saying where he went and why.

bank   chemist's   cinema   hairdresser's
post office   travel agency

book   some medicine
buy   a film
change ─────── a haircut
see   ╲   some money
send   a flight
have   some postcards

Tomek went to the bank to change some money.

UNITS 7-8 REVIEW

8 Complete with the infinitive of these verbs.

> fall get go have wait write

1 Carol promised _____ to Jack.
2 Would you like _____ a pizza?
3 Ben managed _____ Carol an ice cream.
4 Greg told the group _____ for him.
5 Tomek decided _____ to the cinema.
6 Ben didn't want _____ into the water.

9 Match the beginnings with the endings.

1 When you send someone a text message,
2 If you press the red button,
3 When you add two and two,
4 If you warm up snow,
5 When you scan a picture,

a you get water.
b you see it on your computer screen.
c their mobile makes a noise.
d the TV comes on.
e you get four.

10 Listen and add question tags to ask for agreement.
🎧 Tomek is Polish.

> Tomek is Polish, isn't he?

1 Tomek is Polish.
2 The Great Fire was in 1666.
3 Shakespeare's plays were extremely popular.
4 You're from Switzerland.
5 Tamsin was nervous about singing.
6 We're lost.
7 A big rucksack is annoying.
8 You're pulling my leg.
9 Carol was really angry.
10 We were all at the party.

Vocabulary

11 Complete with these words.

> autograph clap earthquake
> fortune teller inventor journalist
> journey litter pilot primary

1 A _____ is someone who predicts the future.
2 A _____ is someone who writes for a newspaper.
3 A _____ is someone who flies a plane.
4 I asked the star to write her name in my book. Now I've got her _____.
5 Look at all those bits of paper on the ground – what a lot of _____.
6 An _____ is a sudden shaking movement of the ground.
7 The _____ from the hotel to the YTV studios takes about half an hour.
8 At the end of the musical everyone started to _____.
9 An _____ is someone who has made, designed or thought of something for the first time.
10 Red and blue are _____ colours.

12 Match these words with their definitions.

> animated films celebrity check-out
> equipment grass luxury sled
> storyboard technique

1 way of doing something using a skill
2 something you use to travel across snow or ice
3 something you enjoy but do not really need
4 series of pictures showing scenes from a film
5 someone who is very well-known, perhaps from TV
6 where you pay in a supermarket
7 machines or things you need to do a job
8 they use moving models or drawings, not actors
9 very common plant with thin green leaves – you can sit on it!

13 Match the verbs in list A with the phrases in list B.

A	B
1 arrive	a technique
2 bring	time
3 catch	on time
4 enter	something to life
5 lay	a competition
6 learn	a train
7 make	the table
8 send	a calculation
9 spend	your feelings
10 show	a text message

14 Find the odd word.

1 fortune teller pilot journalist cinema
2 teacher theatre doctor producer
3 matches candles mirror paraffin
4 tasks insects worms snakes
5 husky reindeer pixel tortoise

PROGRESS CHECK

Now you can...

1 Express obligation and prohibition
2 Express obligation and lack of obligation
3 Make suggestions and express preferences
4 Describe a process
5 Express purpose and consequence
6 Talk about cause and effect
7 Describe how things work
8 Ask for agreement

Look back at Units 7 and 8 and write an example for 1–8.

1 *You mustn't smoke in the YTV studio.*

How good are you? Tick a box.
★★★ Fine ☐   ★★ OK ☐   ★ Not sure ☐

Not sure about something?
Look back through the lesson again.

CONGRATULATIONS!

You've finished *Inspiration 2*. Well done! Now take some time to think about what you have learnt. Let's start with grammar and vocabulary.

★ Grammar

You've revised the grammar you already knew. And you've met and practised new grammar points. Look through the Grammar Summary to see how much you've done.

★ Vocabulary

The Word List shows you all the new words in *Inspiration 2*. The Contents pages list all the vocabulary areas you've covered. Choose some topics (eg Jobs, Buildings) and write a list of all the words you can remember for each one.

But you've learnt more than grammar and vocabulary. In *Inspiration 2* you've also learnt to communicate.

★ Communication

You can …
Describe where people are and what they are doing
Ask and answer questions about people's jobs
Talk about carnivals and festivals
Say what people should and shouldn't do in your country
Interview people about what they love/hate doing
Interview people about what they did last weekend
Talk about the life of a famous person
Ask and answer questions about history
Say what you think will happen next
Describe your favourite TV programme
Talk about your holiday plans
Ask for and give directions to places
Order a meal in a restaurant
Exchange information about experiences
Say what's good and bad about your town
Ask about rules
Talk about a trip
Give definitions of words
Describe someone's character
Describe a process

What else can you do?

You've also developed other language skills.

★ Writing

You can write …
A description of a photo
A personal profile
Notes about a famous person
A description of a place in your country
A poem
A diary entry
Notes and a description of the life of a famous person
Information about the history of your town
A letter about your holiday plans
A description of a TV programme and a character in it
A postcard
Directions from school to your home
A dialogue between a customer and a waiter
A list of rules
An email in reply to an invitation
A description of a journey
Information for visitors to your country
A process description

What else can you write?

★ Listening

You can listen to and understand …
An interview about making a film
An interview about personal likes and dislikes
A description of a celebration
A song
A conversation about recent activities
A story of an accident
A description of the life of a famous person
Drama exercises
Information about changes to a schedule
A conversation about holiday plans
An interview about recent activities
A video commentary about city sights
A description of a famous statue
The rules of a competition
A description of a trip
A conversation between friends at a party

What else can you listen to and understand?

You've also developed another very important skill.

★ Learner Independence

You have learnt …
Ways of finding the meaning of words
How to keep a personal phrasebook
Ways of learning words
How to assess your own progress
How to learn words through word association
How to group and remember words by topic
How words can make word combinations
Words we use to describe grammar
What 'knowing' a word means
The abbreviations we find in a dictionary
How to organise vocabulary
How to assess each other's progress
Different learning strategies
How to define words
Different resources for practice

How do you feel?

Have a class discussion about your English lessons and *Inspiration 2*.

Talk about
- Three things you liked about the lessons and the book
- Activities and exercises you would like to do more often
- Activities and exercises you would like to do less often
- Something you would like to change
- What you would like to do in your English lessons next year

Now write a letter to your teacher giving your opinions.

★ Reading

You can read …
A quiz
An article with personal information
A sketch
A sightseeing guide
An article about carnivals
A questionnaire
An article about a historical event
A biography of a famous person
An article about the history of a city
A magazine article about TV programmes
A schedule about the weekend's arrangements
A menu
A travel guide with tips for backpackers
An article about famous places
A guide to a museum
A description of a tourist attraction
An article about body language
An article about animated films
A story

What else can you read?

COMMUNICATION ACTIVITIES
STUDENT A

UNIT 1

Look at the picture. You know four people in the group.

1 Javier Espinosa, Spanish tennis player
2 Mario Mendes, Portuguese actor
3 Betsy Duncan, Australian swimmer
4 Sophia Andretti, Italian film producer

Ask Student B about the other people. Describe them and find out:

- their names
- their nationalities
- their jobs

Now answer Student B's questions.

Who's the man/woman on the left/ on the right/in the middle? He/She's wearing ...

Where does he/she come from?

What's his/her job?

UNIT 2

Ask Student B questions to find out where these places are.

travel agency   supermarket   chemist's   café   hairdresser's

Where's the travel agency?

Now answer Student B's questions about five more places.

The newsagent's is opposite the restaurant.

HOTEL   BOOKSHOP   NEWSAGENT'S   POLICE STATION

FLOWER SHOP   POST OFFICE   RESTAURANT   BANK   CINEMA

STUDENT A

UNIT 3

Read the text. Then ask Student B questions to complete it. Answer Student B's questions.

> When did the Romans come to England?

THE HISTORY OF LONDON

The Romans came to England in __1__ (when?) and built the town of Londinium on the River Thames. Londinium soon grew bigger and bigger. Ships came there from all over Europe and the Romans built __2__ (what?) from Londinium to other parts of Britain. By the year 400, there were 50,000 people in the city.

Soon after 400 the Romans left, and we do not know much about London between 400 and 1000. In __3__ (when?) William the Conqueror came to England from Normandy in France. William became King of England and lived in __4__ (where?). But William was afraid of the people of London, so he built a big building for himself – the White Tower. Now it is part of the Tower of London and many __5__ (who?) visit it to see the Crown Jewels – the Queen's gold and diamonds.

London continued to grow. By 1600 there were __6__ (how many?) people in the city and by 1830 the population was one and a half million people. The railways came and there were __7__ (what?) all over the city. This was the London that Dickens knew and wrote about – a city of very rich and very poor people.

At the start of the twentieth century, __8__ (how many?) people lived in London. Today the population of Greater London is seven and a half million. __9__ (how many?) tourists visit London every year and you can hear 300 different languages on London's streets!

UNIT 4

Sally and Jack are talking about their holiday plans. You are Sally and Student B is Jack. The sentences in the box are Sally's part of the conversation. But the sentences are not in the right order.

> But what do you really want to do?
> Don't forget – summer in Europe is winter in Australia!
> What are you going to do in the summer holidays?
> Great. You can come and visit me.
> I'm going to go skiing.

Work with Student B to put the conversation in the right order. Don't look at Student B's sentences. You start the conversation.

UNIT 5

Kate and Greg are talking about the arrangements for tomorrow. You are Kate and Student B is Greg. Kate wants to record a 15-minute interview with Tomek and Gabi. Read Kate's diary and ask Student B questions to find the best time for the interview.

> I'm meeting the new actors at nine o'clock but I'm free at ten. What are Tomek and Gabi doing at ten?

28 August
Interview Tomek and Gabi?

9am	Meet the new actors at YTV
10am	Free
10.30am	Record the quiz programme
12-1pm	Free
1-2pm	Have lunch with TV producer
2-3pm	Rehearse
3-4.30pm	Free
4.30-5.30pm	Watch this morning's recording
5.30pm	Free
6pm	Read the news
6.30-7.45pm	Free
7.45pm	Go to the cinema

107

STUDENT A

UNIT 6

Ask Student B questions to complete the chart.

A Has Gabi ever been on TV?
B Yes, she has.
A How many times has she been on TV?
B Twice.

	Ben	Gabi	Laura	Tomek	Sally	Pedro
be on TV	1		2			0
visit Los Angeles		0		0	1	
win a competition	2		3			1
fall in love		2	5		0	
make a cake	0		10	2		
fly in a plane	4	6			10	6

Now look at the chart and answer Student B's questions.

B Has Ben ever been on TV?
A Yes, he has.
B How many times has he been on TV?
A Once.

UNIT 7

Give definitions of these nouns to Student B, but don't say the word.

> Number 1. It means 'two weeks'.

1 fortnight
2 luxury
3 matches
4 insect
5 exhibition
6 environment

Now listen to Student B's definitions of these nouns. If you guess the word, write it down, but don't say it.

7   _ u _ _ _ v _ _
8   _ _ p t _ _ _
9   r _ _ _ d _ _ _
10 _ _ _ f _ r _
11 r _ _ n _ _ _ _ s _
12 t _ _ _ _ r _ _ _ r _

Then check your answers with Student B.

UNIT 8

Student B has the missing words from this crossword. You have Student B's missing words. Don't say the words! Take turns to ask each other for clues and try to complete the crossword.

> What's 1 down?

> It's someone who works for a newspaper.

> What's 1 across?

> It's a short coat.

108

GRAMMAR SUMMARY

Present simple: be
UNIT 1 THIS IS YTV

Affirmative		Questions
Full forms	Contractions	
I am	I'm	am I?
you are	you're	are you?
he is	he's	is he?
she is	she's	is she?
it is	it's	is it?
we are	we're	are we?
you are	you're	are you?
they are	they're	are they?

Negative	
I am not	I'm not
you are not	you aren't
he is not	he isn't
she is not	she isn't
it is not	it isn't
we are not	we aren't
you are not	you aren't
they are not	they aren't

- In questions with the verb *be*, the verb comes before the subject:
    Are you English?
    Where is Pedro from?
- We make the negative by adding *not*.
- We use the full form in affirmative short answers and the contraction in negative short answers:
    Yes, she is.   No, she isn't.

Present simple
UNIT 1 LESSONS 1 AND 3

Affirmative	Negative	
	Full forms	Contractions
I like	I do not like	I don't like
you like	you do not like	you don't like
he likes	he does not like	he doesn't like
she likes	she does not like	she doesn't like
it likes	it does not like	it doesn't like
we like	we do not like	we don't like
you like	you do not like	you don't like
they like	they do not like	they don't like

Questions	Short answers	
Do you like...?	Yes, I do.	No, I don't.
	Yes, we do.	No, we don't.
Does he like...?	Yes, he does.	No, he doesn't.
Does she like...?	Yes, she does.	No, she doesn't.
Does it like...?	Yes, it does.	No, it doesn't.
Do they like...?	Yes, they do.	No, they don't.

- We use the present simple to describe states, routines, timetables and regular actions:
    I go to the movies on Saturdays.
    She loves pigeons.
    Carol speaks Italian.
    What languages do you speak?
    Do you really speak Chinese?
    I don't play on my computer.
    She doesn't speak Chinese.
- We use the present simple to talk about what people do in their jobs and occupations:
    What do you do? (= What's your job?)
    I'm a TV producer.
    I make sure that the film is good.
- The verb does not change in the present simple affirmative except after *he, she, it*:
    he live**s**   she live**s**   it live**s**
- Present simple negative: subject + *do/does not* + verb:
    He doesn't play on his computer.
- Present simple questions: *do/does* + subject + verb.
  In *does* questions, the main verb does not end in *s*:
    Does she like̸ computers?

Present continuous
UNIT 1 LESSONS 2 AND 3, UNIT 5 LESSON 1

Affirmative	
Full forms	Contractions
I am talking	I'm talking
you are talking	you're talking
he is talking	he's talking
she is talking	she's talking
it is talking	it's talking
we are talking	we're talking
you are talking	you're talking
they are talking	they're talking

Negative	
I am not talking	I'm not talking
you are not talking	you aren't/you're not talking
he is not talking	he isn't/he's not talking
she is not talking	she isn't/she's not talking
it is not talking	it isn't/it's not talking
we are not talking	we aren't/we're not talking
you are not talking	you aren't/you're not talking
they are not talking	they aren't/they're not talking

Questions	Short answers
Are you talking?	Yes, I am.
	No, I'm not.
	Yes, we are.
	No, we aren't. No, we're not.
Is he/she/it talking?	Yes, he/she/it is.
	No, he/she/it isn't.
	No, he's/she's/it's not.
Are they talking?	Yes, they are.
	No, they aren't. No, they're not.

109

GRAMMAR SUMMARY

- We use the present continuous to talk about temporary events and what is happening now:
    You're standing on my foot.
    He's wearing a YTV badge.
    They're holding hands.
    What are they doing?
    Is he helping her?
    He isn't helping her.
    They aren't holding hands.
- We can also use the present continuous to talk about future arrangements, and we often say the time and/or place:
    Greg is taking people to the Science Museum.
    We're returning to the hotel at 5.30pm.
    They aren't having lunch at the hotel.
    What time are they having lunch?
    Who is taking them to the Science Museum?
    How long are they spending at the museums?
- **Spelling:** verb + -ing
    Most verbs add -ing:
    stand – standing   hold – holding
    Verbs ending in -e drop the -e and add -ing:
    take – taking   leave – leaving
    Other verbs:
    swim – swimming   run – running
    put – putting   sit – sitting

Possessive adjectives and Possessive pronouns
UNIT 1 LESSON 3

Possessive adjectives		Possessive pronouns	
my	our	mine	ours
your	your	yours	yours
his/her	their	his/hers	theirs

- Possessive adjectives do not change with plural nouns:
    my book   **my** book**s**
- We do not use *the* before possessive pronouns:
    *This book is ~~the~~ **mine**.*
- We use the question word *Whose* to ask about possession:
    Whose are the glasses?
    Whose is this book? OR *Whose book is this?*

Possessive forms: 's and s'
UNIT 1 LESSON 3

- Singular nouns add *'s* (apostrophe *s*):
    the producer's job   Kate's boots
- Plural nouns add *s'*:
    the actors' coffee break   the girls' bags
- Irregular plural nouns add *'s*:
    people's pockets   the women's bags

Comparative and superlative adjectives
UNIT 2 LESSON 1

Adjective 1 syllable	Comparative	Superlative
small	smaller	the smallest
large	larger	the largest

1 syllable ending in single vowel + single consonant		
big	bigger	the biggest
hot	hotter	the hottest

2 syllables ending in -y		
noisy	noisier	the noisiest
silly	sillier	the silliest

2 or more syllables		
famous	more famous	the most famous
exciting	more exciting	the most exciting

Irregular		
good	better	the best
bad	worse	the worst

- Some two-syllable adjectives add -er/est or -r/st:
    clever   cleverer   the cleverest
    simple   simpler   simplest
- The opposite of *more* is *less*:
    It's less expensive than Rio!
- The opposite of *most* is *least*:
    They stayed in the least expensive hotel.

should/shouldn't
UNIT 2 LESSON 2

- We can use *should* and *shouldn't* (*should not*) to express advice:
    We should stay together.
    You should tell me where you're going.
    You shouldn't go off on your own.
    Why should they tell Greg?
- *should* is a modal auxiliary verb:
    – it does not change with *he/she/it*.
    – there is no *to* between *should* and the main verb:
    You should ~~to~~ take flowers.

110

GRAMMAR SUMMARY

Prepositions of place
UNIT 2 LESSON 2

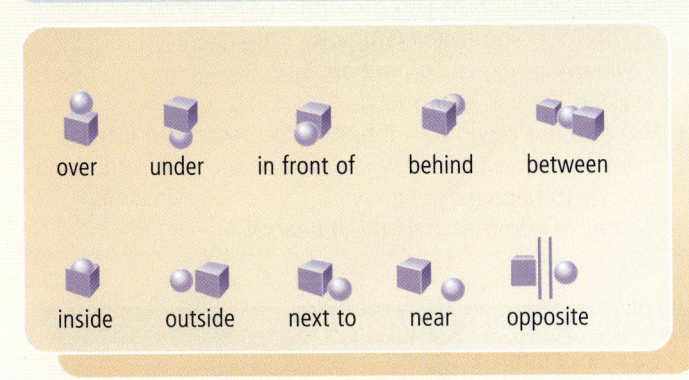

over under in front of behind between

inside outside next to near opposite

- *in front of* is the opposite of *behind*:
  Ben can't see because Carol is **in front of** him.
- *opposite* means *facing*:
  Page 21 is **opposite** page 20.

The gerund (*-ing* form)
UNIT 2 LESSON 3

- A gerund is a noun formed from a verb. We can use a gerund after *like, love, hate, enjoy,* and *can't stand*:
  I love go**ing** to festivals.
  I hate be**ing** lost.
  I don't enjoy be**ing** rude.
  I can't stand wait**ing** for people.
  What do you like do**ing**?
- We can also use a gerund after prepositions:
  You're good **at** danc**ing**.
  I'm not interested **in** listen**ing** to bossy people.

Past simple
UNIT 3 LESSONS 1 AND 2

be

Affirmative	Negative
I/he/she/it was	I/he/she/it wasn't (was not)
we/you/they were	we/you/they weren't (were not)

Questions	Short answers
Were you ...?	Yes, I was.
	No, I wasn't.
	Yes, we were.
	No, we weren't.
Was he/she/it ...?	Yes, he/she/it was.
	No, he/she/it wasn't.
Were they ...?	Yes, they were.
	No, they weren't.

- There are only two past simple forms of *be*:
  Everything was very dry.
  The people were asleep.
  The fire wasn't near his house.
  There weren't many buildings left.
- In questions, the subject comes after *was/were*:
  Was Jack asleep all morning?
  Were they exhausted?

Regular verbs

Affirmative	Negative
I	I
you	you
he/she/it started	he/she/it didn't start
we	we (did not start)
you	you
they	they

Questions	Short answers
Did you start?	Yes, I/we did.
	No, I/we didn't. (did not)
Did he/she/it start?	Yes, he/she/it did.
	No, he/she/it didn't. (did not)
Did they start?	Yes, they did.
	No, they didn't. (did not)

- **Spelling:** affirmative forms of regular verbs
  Most verbs add *-ed*:
    start – start**ed**   destroy – destroy**ed**
  Verbs ending in *-e* add *d*:
    escape – escape**d**   die – die**d**
  Verbs ending in a consonant and *-y* drop the *-y* and add *-ied*:
    car**y** – car**ried**   mar**y** – mar**ried**
- Past simple negative: subject + *didn't* + verb:
  The fire didn't cross the river.
- Past simple questions: *did* + subject + verb:
  What did you do?
  How/When did they cross the river?
  Did you have fun?
  Did they see a play?

Irregular verbs
- There is a complete list of all the irregular verbs in *Inspiration 2* on page 127.
- Irregular verbs form the negative and questions in the same way as regular verbs:
  They didn't have time to take a lot with them.

Adverbial phrases of time
UNIT 3 LESSON 2

- We use *on* for days and dates:
  on Saturday (morning)   on 21 August
- We use *in* for periods during the day (except *night*), months and years:
  in the morning   in August   in 1666
- We use *at* for specific times:
  at 9am   at noon/midnight
  and in certain fixed expressions:
  at night   at the weekend

111

GRAMMAR SUMMARY

Past continuous
UNIT 3 LESSON 3

Affirmative	Negative
I/he/she/it was listening	I/he/she/it wasn't listening
we/you/they were listening	we/you/they weren't listening

Questions	Short answers
Were you listening?	Yes, I was.
	No, I wasn't.
	Yes, we were.
	No, we weren't.
Was he/she/it listening?	Yes, he/she/it was.
	No, he/she/it wasn't.
Were they listening?	Yes, they were.
	No, they weren't.

- We use the past continuous to describe what was happening at a particular time in the past, to give the background to an event:

  At 2.30pm
  ← – – – we were passing the London Eye. – – – →

- We form the past continuous with *was/were* + *-ing* form:
  - I was listening to Greg
  - I wasn't looking
  - She was taking photos
  - We were passing the London Eye

  when Ben fell in.
  at 2.30pm.

  What was he doing? What were you doing?
  Was he feeling all right?

Why ...? because (reason)
UNIT 3 LESSON 3

- We use the conjunction *because* to answer the question *Why...?*
  Why did Sally shout 'Help!'?
  She shouted 'Help!' **because** Ben fell overboard.

going to
UNIT 4 LESSON 1

Affirmative	Negative
I'm	I'm not
you're	you aren't/you're not
he's	he isn't/he's not
she's going to	she isn't/she's not going to
it's	it isn't/it's not
we're	we aren't/we're not
they're	they aren't/they're not

Questions	Short answers
Are you going to?	Yes, I am. Yes, we are.
	No, I'm not. No, we aren't.
	No, we're not.
Is he/she/it going to?	Yes, he/she/it is.
	No, he/she/it isn't.
	No, he's/she's/it's not.
Are they going to?	Yes, they are.
	No, they aren't. No, they're not.

- We use *going to* + infinitive to talk about future plans and intentions:
  I'm going to take you on a tour of the studio.
  I'm not going to tell you now.
  Are we going to be here all day?
  What are you going to do?

- We also use *going to* + infinitive to predict the future from present evidence, when we can see that something is likely to happen:
  They're going to start the rehearsal.

Future simple: will/won't
UNIT 4 LESSON 2

- We can use *will* and *won't* (*will not*) to say what we hope or predict about the future:
  I'll miss working with Liam.
  We'll see each other again.
  I won't have anyone to talk to.
  What will Simon do with the gun?
  Will Robbie escape?

- *will* is a modal auxiliary verb:
  – it does not change with *he/she/it*.
  I think he will escape.
  He won't be in Westsiders after this week's episode.
  – there is no *to* between *will* and the main verb.
  I hope he'll ~~to~~ keep in touch.

Adverbs of manner
UNIT 4 LESSON 3

Regular		Irregular	
Adjective	Adverb	Adjective	Adverb
bad	bad**ly**	early	early
normal	normal**ly**	fast	fast
proper	proper**ly**	good	well
quick	quick**ly**	hard	hard
proper	proper**ly**	late	late
quick	quick**ly**		
comforta**ble**	comforta**bly**		
angr**y**	angr**ily**		
happ**y**	happ**ily**		

- We use adverbs of manner to describe **how** we do something:
  You spoke too fast.
  Actors work really hard.

- **Spelling:**
  Most adjectives add *-ly*:
  *normal – normal**ly**   proper – proper**ly***
  Adjectives ending in *-y* drop the y and add *-ily*:
  *happ**y** – happ**ily**   angr**y** – angr**ily***
  Adjectives ending in *-ble* drop the *-e* and add *-y*:
  *comforta**ble** – comforta**bly**   terri**ble** – terri**bly***

112

GRAMMAR SUMMARY

Sequencing adverbs
UNIT 5 LESSON 1

First they're visiting London Zoo.
Next they're walking along the Regent's Canal.
Then they're having lunch.
After that, they're going shopping.
Finally they're taking a canal boat trip.

- We use sequencing adverbs to describe a sequence of events. We can use *next, then*, and *after that* in any order.
- We always put a comma after *after that*.

Object pronouns
UNIT 5 LESSON 2

Singular	Plural
me	us
you	you
him, her, it	them

- We use object pronouns after verbs and prepositions:
    I can show **him** the way.
    Can you help **us**?
    Listen to **me**.
    I'm waiting for **him**.

Verb + indirect and direct object
UNIT 5 LESSON 2

- Many verbs can have two objects:
    I'll give you a map.
    (*you* = indirect object; *a map* = direct object)
    I'll ask her the way.
    (*her* = indirect object; *the way* = direct object)
- The following verbs can have indirect and direct objects:
    ask bring buy give send sing take write
- The indirect object with a preposition can come after the direct object:
    She bought a present **for him**.
    I'll give the map **to you**.

Prepositions of direction
UNIT 5 LESSON 2

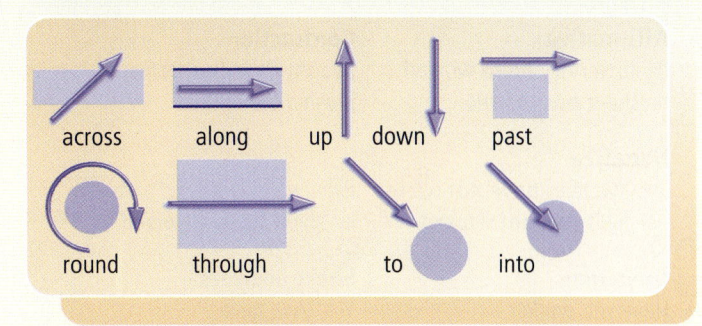

across   along   up   down   past
round   through   to   into

- Note these examples with *across* and *through*:

	the bridge		the trees
	the river		the crowd
across	the street	**through**	the door
	the room		the window
	the road		the rain

- We often use *down*, and sometimes *up*, to mean *along* when there is no hill!
    We ran **down the road** to the bus stop.
    He walked **up the path** to the front door.

some and *any*
UNIT 5 LESSON 3

- We use *some* and *any* with both plural and uncountable nouns.
- We use *some* in affirmative sentences, and in requests and questions when we want/expect the answer 'yes':
    I'd like some garlic bread.
    Could I borrow some money?
- We use *any* in negative sentences and neutral questions:
    I don't want any olives/meat.
    Have you got any pizzas with mushrooms?

How much/many?
UNIT 5 LESSON 3

- We use *How much . . .?* with uncountable nouns:
    How much money have you got?
    How much bread do you want?
- We use *How many . . .?* with plural countable nouns:
    How many colas?
    How many people are there?

Countable and uncountable nouns
UNIT 5 LESSON 3

- Countable nouns have a singular and a plural form:
    a tomato – tomatoes   an olive – olives
- We don't use *a/an* with uncountable nouns:
    We like cheese.   Do you want some bread?
- Uncountable nouns are singular:
    It's rice.   Spaghetti **comes** from Italy.

GRAMMAR SUMMARY

Present perfect
UNIT 6 LESSONS 1 AND 2

Affirmative
I/you/we/they **have** worked
he/she/it **has** worked

Contractions
I/you/we/they**'ve** worked
he/she/it**'s** worked

Negative
I/you/we/they **have not** worked
he/she/it **has not** worked
I/you/we/they **haven't** worked
he/she/it **hasn't** worked

Questions
Have you worked?

Has he/she/it worked?

Have they worked?

Short answers
Yes, I/we have.
No, I/we haven't.
Yes, he/she/it has.
No she/she/it hasn't.
Yes, they have.
No, they haven't.

- We can use the present perfect to talk about recent completed actions or events.
    I have tried to talk to her.
    She has been horrible to me.
    Have you recorded anything?
    Yes, I have.
    Have you had an argument with her?
    No, I haven't.
    What has Carol recorded?
  We don't say the exact time of the action or event, but we can refer to an unfinished period of time, for example *all day, today, this week/month/year*.
    She hasn't said a word to me all day.
    Have you had fun this week?
- We can use the present perfect with *just* to talk about very recent events:
    I've just worked out how to use the camera.
    I've just filmed you two.
- We can also use the present perfect, often with *ever/never*, to talk about experiences at an indefinite time in the past.
- *ever* = *at any time*. It is used mainly in questions:
    Have you ever felt really stupid?
    Have you ever had a girlfriend?
- *ever* is also used in affirmative statements after superlatives:
    It's the best film I've ever seen.
- *never* = at no time:
    I've never been so embarrassed.
    She has never seen anyone so angry before.
- We form the present perfect with *have/has* + past participle.
- For regular verbs the past participle is the same as the past tense: *work, worked, worked*
- For some irregular verbs the past participle is the same as the past tense, but for many it is different: *be, was/were, been*. There is a complete list of all the irregular verbs in *Inspiration 2* on page 127.
- The past participle of *go* can be *gone* or *been* (= *gone and returned*):
    He's gone to Rio. = *He's in Rio now.*
    He's been to Rio. = *He's visited Rio but he's not there now.*

too much/too many and (not) enough
UNIT 6 LESSON 3

- We use *too much* with uncountable nouns:
    They cost too much money.
    Don't make too much noise.
- We use *too many* with plural countable nouns:
    There are too many tourists.
    There are too many queues.
- We put *enough* before nouns:
    There isn't enough time.
  and after adjectives and adverbs:
    Is that loud enough?

must and mustn't
UNIT 7 LESSON 1

- We use *must* to express present and future obligation, often when talking about rules:
    The celebrities must give up luxuries.
    They must learn survival techniques.
    What kind of things must they do?
- We use *mustn't* (*must not*) for prohibition:
    They mustn't take mobile phones.
    They mustn't forget the dangers of the jungle.
- *must* is a modal auxiliary verb:
    – it does not change with *he/she/it*.
    – there is no *to* between *must* and the main verb.
    They must ~~to~~ eat insects and worms.
- The past tense of *must* is *had to*:
    One person had to walk through water full of crocodiles.
- *must* is stronger than *should*.

have/has to and don't/doesn't have to
UNIT 7 LESSON 2

- We also use *have/has to* to talk about present and future obligation:
    I have to do some shopping.
    Carol has to buy some presents.
    Do we have to go?
- We use *don't/doesn't have to* to express lack of obligation:
    You don't have to come with me.
- *have to* and *must* in the affirmative both express obligation. But:
    – *don't/doesn't have to* = It's not necessary.
    – *mustn't* = It's not allowed.
- The past tense of both *must* and *have to* is *had to*:
    We had to stay there for ages.

GRAMMAR SUMMARY

Participial adjectives ending in -ed/-ing
UNIT 7 LESSON 3

- Adjectives ending in -ed describe a feeling or reaction:
    You'll be surprised by the human body.
    Don't be frightened!
- Adjectives ending in -ing describe the **cause** of the feeling or reaction:
    There are lots of surprising fish.
    Earthquakes are shocking.
- The following are common participial adjectives:

amazed – amazing	bored – boring	excited – exciting
fascinated – fascinating	frightened – frightening	
interested – interesting	shocked – shocking	
surprised – surprising	tired – tiring	

Infinitive of purpose
UNIT 8 LESSON 1

- We use the infinitive of purpose to say **why** we do something:
    They use models to make the films.
    Nick Park joined the studio to work on a film.
    The animator uses the storyboard to plan the film.

Verb + infinitive
UNIT 8 LESSON 1

- We use *to* + infinitive after certain verbs:
    The BBC offered to buy one of their first films.
    They decided to call it Aardman.
    They often only manage to make three seconds of film.
- We can use *to* + infinitive after these verbs and phrases:

agree	ask	decide	know how	learn	manage
mean	need	offer	pretend	promise	refuse
seem	teach	tell	want	would like	

Open conditional with *if/when*
UNIT 8 LESSON 2

- We use the open conditional to talk about cause and effect:
    If you like a boy, you're rude.
    When I'm on my own, I get depressed.
    When we mix red and green, we get yellow.
- In open conditional sentences, both verbs are in the present simple tense:
- The *if/when* clause can follow the main clause:
    I don't like it when people tell me what to do.
    What do you do if people are bossy?
    How do you feel when you're on your own?

Question tags
UNIT 8 LESSON 3

- We can use question tags with **falling** intonation to ask for agreement when we are sure about something:
    It's my job, **isn't it**?
    You're an expert on London, **aren't you**?
    They're celebrating Chinese New Year, **aren't they**?
    It was a long time, **wasn't it**?
    The questions were quite easy, **weren't they**?
- When the statement in the first part of the sentence is affirmative, the question tag is negative.
- We can use question tags with **rising** intonation to ask real questions:
    It's nearly 7 o'clock, **isn't it**?

Conjunctions

- We use **and** to connect two similar ideas:
    Tomek really likes music and he loves hip-hop.
- We use **but** to connect two contrasting ideas:
    Ben was shivering, but he was laughing.
- We use **or** to connect two alternative ideas:
    Will Simon tie Robbie up, or will Robbie escape?
- We use **because** to talk about reason or cause:
    Ben wants to be a pilot because he likes flying.
- We use **so** to talk about consequence or result.
    Ben likes flying, so he wants to be a pilot.

115

COMMUNICATION ACTIVITIES
STUDENT B

UNIT 1

Look at the picture. You know four people in the group.

5 Carmen García, Argentinian tourist guide
6 Julie Christmas, British stuntwoman
7 Rolf Braun, German singer
8 Carlos Costa, Brazilian director

Answer Student A's questions about them.

Now ask Student A about the other people. Describe them and find out:

- their names
- their nationalities
- their jobs

> Who's the man/woman on the left/on the right/in the middle? He/She's wearing ...

> Where does he/she come from?

> What's his/her job?

UNIT 2

Answer Student A's questions about five places.

> The travel agency is opposite the hotel.

Now ask Student A questions to find out where these places are.

newsagent's   police station   bank   post office   flower shop

> Where's the newsagent's?

HOTEL   HAIRDRESSER'S   BOOKSHOP   CHEMIST'S   SUPERMARKET

TRAVEL AGENCY   CAFÉ   RESTAURANT   CINEMA

116

STUDENT B

UNIT 3

Read the text. Then ask Student A questions to complete it. Answer Student A's questions.

> Where did the Romans build Londinium?

THE HISTORY OF LONDON

The Romans came to England in AD43 and built the town of Londinium __10__ (where?). Londinium soon grew bigger and bigger. __11__ (what?) came there from all over Europe and the Romans built roads from Londinium to other parts of Britain. By the year 400, there were __12__ (how many?) people in the city.

Soon after __13__ (when?) the Romans left, and we do not know much about London between 400 and 1000. In 1066 William the Conqueror came to England from __14__ (where?). William became King of England and lived in London. But William was afraid of __15__ (who?) so he built a big building for himself – the White Tower. Now it is part of the Tower of London and many tourists visit it to see the Crown Jewels – the Queen's gold and diamonds.

London continued to grow. By 1600 there were 200,000 people in the city and by __16__ (when?) the population was one and a half million people. The railways came and there were factories all over the city. This was the London that Dickens knew and wrote about – a city of very rich and very poor people.

At the start of the twentieth century, four and a half million people lived in London. Today the population of Greater London is __17__ (what?). Twenty-six million tourists visit London every year and you can hear __18__ (how many?) different languages on London's streets!

UNIT 4

Jack and Sally are talking about their holiday plans. You are Jack and Student A is Sally. The sentences in the box are Jack's part of the conversation. But the sentences are not in the right order.

> What, in the summer?
> I don't know. My parents are going to Spain, so I'll probably go with them.
> Thank you!
> What are you going to do in the summer holidays?
> I really want to go to Australia.
> Of course. How stupid of me!

Work with Student A to put the conversation in the right order. Don't look at Student A's sentences. Student A starts the conversation.

UNIT 5

Greg and Kate are talking about the arrangements for tomorrow. You are Greg and Student A is Kate. Kate wants to record a 15-minute interview with Tomek and Gabi. Read 'What's happening tomorrow' and work with Student A to find the best time for the interview.

> No, I'm afraid ten o'clock is no good. They're leaving the hotel at ten. How about one o'clock?

What's happening tomorrow?

10am-1pm	Leave hotel and take the underground to Tower Hill
	Visit the Tower of London
1-1.30pm	Free
1.30-2.30pm	Have lunch on Tower Bridge
2.30-4.30pm	Visit *The Gazette* newspaper office
4.30-5.30pm	Free
5.30pm	Return to the hotel
6-6.30pm	Free
6.30-7.15pm	Dinner
7.15-8pm	Free
8-10pm	Quiz Night

117

STUDENT B

UNIT 6

Look at the chart and answer Student A's questions.

A Has Gabi ever been on TV?
B Yes, she has.
A How many times has she been on TV?
B Twice.

	Ben	Gabi	Laura	Tomek	Sally	Pedro
be on TV		2		1	0	
visit Los Angeles	1		0			2
win a competition		1	3		2	
fall in love	1			3		0
make a cake		2			1	5
fly in a plane				2	5	

Now ask Student A questions to complete the chart.

B Has Ben ever been on TV?
A Yes, he has.
B How many times has he been on TV?
A Once.

UNIT 7

Listen to Student A's definitions of these nouns. If you guess the word, write it down, but don't say it.

1 _ _ _ t _ _ g _ _
2 _ u _ _ _ y
3 _ _ _ c h _ _
4 _ _ s _ c _
5 e _ _ _ b _ _ _ _ n
6 e _ _ _ r _ _ _ _ n _

Now give definitions of these nouns to Student A, but don't say the word.

> Number 7. It means 'staying alive in a difficult place'.

7 survival
8 reptile
9 reindeer
10 uniform
11 rainforest
12 temperature

Then check your answers with Student A.

UNIT 8

Student A has the missing words from this crossword. You have Student A's missing words. Don't say the words! Take turns to ask each other for clues and try to complete the crossword.

> What's 1 down?
> It's someone who works for a newspaper.
> What's 1 across?
> It's a short coat.

118

WORD LIST

The Word List excludes *Inspiration 1* vocabulary in these categories:
ADVERBS OF FREQUENCY
COLOURS
COUNTRIES, NATIONALITIES and LANGUAGES
DAYS OF THE WEEK and MONTHS
FAMILY
NUMBERS
PARTS OF THE BODY
POSSESSIVE ADJECTIVES and PRONOUNS
TIME and TIMES OF THE DAY

Unit 1

aerobics (n)	/eəˈrəʊbɪks/
again (adv)	/əˈgen/
all right	/ɔːl ˈraɪt/
angry (adj)	/ˈæŋgri/
answer (n)	/ˈɑːnsə/
because (conj) (TS)	/bɪˈkʌz/
bed (n)	/bed/
before (prep)	/bɪˈfɔː/
behind	/bɪˈhaɪnd/
bird (n)	/bɜːd/
birthday (n)	/ˈbɜːθdeɪ/
book (n)	/bʊk/
boss (n)	/bɒs/
boy (n)	/bɔɪ/
boyfriend (n)	/ˈbɔɪfrend/
breakfast (n)	/ˈbrekfəst/
busker (n)	/ˈbʌskə/
buy (v)	/baɪ/
call (v)	/kɔːl/
1 = telephone	
2 = name someone/something	
car crash (n)	/ˈkɑː kræʃ/
in charge of	/ɪn ˈtʃɑːdʒ əv/
chat (v)	/tʃæt/
cinema (n)	/ˈsɪnəmə/
clothes (n)	/kləʊðz/
coffee (n)	/ˈkɒfi/
coffee break (n)	/ˈkɒfi breɪk/
colour (n)	/ˈkʌlə/
come (v)	/kʌm/
competition (n)	/kɒmpəˈtɪʃən/
computer (n)	/kəmˈpjuːtə/
continue (v)	/kənˈtɪnjuː/
correct (adj)	/kəˈrekt/
cycle (v)	/ˈsaɪkəl/
dangerous (adj)	/ˈdeɪndʒərəs/
It depends.	/ɪt dɪˈpendz/
dictionary (n)	/ˈdɪkʃnri/
different (adj)	/ˈdɪfrənt/
difficult (adj)	/ˈdɪfɪkəlt/
dinner (n)	/ˈdɪnə/
dog (n)	/dɒg/
drink (n)	/drɪŋk/
easy (adj)	/ˈiːzi/
eat (v)	/iːt/
evening (n)	/ˈiːvnɪŋ/
every (adj)	/ˈevri/
everyone (pron)	/ˈevriwʌn/
Excuse me.	/ɪkˈskjuːz miː/
expensive (adj)	/ɪkˈspensɪv/
fact (n) (TS)	/fækt/
favourite (adj)	/ˈfeɪvrət/
fight (n)	/faɪt/
film (n)	/fɪlm/
finally (adv)	/ˈfaɪnəli/
find out	/faɪnd ˈaʊt/
first (adv)	/fɜːst/
fish (n)	/fɪʃ/
flower (n)	/ˈflaʊə/
food (n)	/fuːd/
football (n)	/ˈfʊtbɔːl/
for example	/fə(r) ɪkˈzɑːmpəl/
friend (n)	/frend/
from (prep)	/frɒm/
fun (adj)	/fʌn/
garden (n)	/ˈgɑːdən/
girl (n)	/gɜːl/
girlfriend (n)	/ˈgɜːlfrend/
good (adj)	/gʊd/
Goodbye.	/gʊdˈbaɪ/
great (adj)	/greɪt/
group (n)	/gruːp/
guess (v)	/ges/
guitar (n)	/gɪˈtɑː/
half an hour	/hɑːf ən ˈaʊə/
happen (v)	/ˈhæpən/
happy (adj)	/ˈhæpi/
Have a great time.	/hæv ə greɪt ˈtaɪm/
hear (v)	/hɪə/
Hello.	/heˈləʊ/
help (n & v)	/help/
hip-hop (n)	/ˈhɪp hɒp/
hold (v)	/həʊld/
hold hands	/həʊld ˈhændz/
holiday(s) (n)	/ˈhɒlɪdeɪ(z)/
at home	/ət ˈhəʊm/
hope (v)	/həʊp/
hotel (n)	/həʊˈtel/
How about …?	/haʊ əbaʊt/
important (adj)	/ɪmˈpɔːtənt/
job (n)	/dʒɒb/
joke (n)	/dʒəʊk/
kilometre (km) (n)	/ˈkɪlɒmɪtə/
know (v)	/nəʊ/
language (n)	/ˈlæŋgwɪdʒ/
late (adv)	/leɪt/
learn (v)	/lɜːn/
leave (v)	/liːv/
left (adj)	/left/
Let me see.	/let miː ˈsiː/
light (n)	/laɪt/
like (v)	/laɪk/
listen (v)	/ˈlɪsən/
live (v)	/lɪv/
look (v)	/lʊk/
look forward to	/lʊk ˈfɔːwəd tə/
lots of	/lɒts əv/
love (v)	/lʌv/
magazine (n)	/mægəˈziːn/
make a film	/meɪk ə ˈfɪlm/
make sure	/meɪk ˈʃʊə/
man (n) (pl men)	/mæn/ (/men/)
map (n)	/mæp/
mean (v)	/miːn/
meet (v)	/miːt/
miss (v)	/mɪs/
(miss someone)	
mistake (n)	/mɪsˈteɪk/
at the moment	/ət ðə ˈməʊmənt/
move (v)	/muːv/
movie (n)	/ˈmuːvi/
music (n)	/ˈmjuːzɪk/
name (n)	/neɪm/
next to	/ˈneks tə/
notebook (n)	/ˈnəʊtbʊk/
nothing (pron)	/ˈnʌθɪŋ/
of course (not)	/əv ˈkɔːs (nɒt)/
online (adv)	/ˈɒnlaɪn/
Pardon?	/ˈpɑːdən/
part (= role) (n)	/pɑːt/
passenger (n)	/ˈpæsɪndʒə/
person (pl people) (n)	/ˈpɜːsən/ (/ˈpiːpəl/)
phone (v)	/fəʊn/
pickpocket (n)	/ˈpɪkpɒkɪt/
pigeon (n)	/ˈpɪdʒɪn/
play (music) (v)	/pleɪ (ˈmjuːzɪk)/
play (a role) (v)	/pleɪ (ə rəʊl)/
play (sport) (v)	/pleɪ (spɔːt)/
pocket (n)	/ˈpɒkɪt/
point (n)	/pɔɪnt/
population (n)	/pɒpjʊˈleɪʃən/
prize (n)	/praɪz/
problem (n)	/ˈprɒbləm/
put (v)	/pʊt/
quick (adv)	/kwɪk/
rap (music) (n)	/ræp/
read (v)	/riːd/
relax (v)	/rɪˈlæks/
remember (v) (TS)	/rɪˈmembə/
right	/raɪt/
1 = correct (adj)	
2 = on the right (n)	
river (n)	/ˈrɪvə/
run (v)	/rʌn/
sandwich (n)	/ˈsændwɪdʒ/
sea monster (n)	/ˈsiː mɒnstə/
seat (n)	/siːt/
see (v)	/siː/
sell (v)	/sel/
ship (n)	/ʃɪp/
shoot (a film) (v)	/ʃuːt/
short (adj)	/ʃɔːt/
for short	/fə ˈʃɔːt/
sightseeing (n)	/ˈsaɪtsiːɪŋ/
silly (adj)	/ˈsɪli/
sir	/sɜː/
sit (v)	/sɪt/
someone (pron)	/ˈsʌmwʌn/
sorry (adj)	/ˈsɒri/
speak (v)	/spiːk/
special (adj)	/ˈspeʃəl/
spell (v)	/spel/
square (n)	/skweə/
stand (v)	/stænd/
star (n)	/stɑː/
station (n)	/ˈsteɪʃən/
stay (v)	/steɪ/
steal (v)	/stiːl/
stop (v)	/stɒp/
stunt (n) (TS)	/stʌnt/
sugar (n)	/ˈʃʊgə/
summer (n)	/ˈsʌmə/
sunshine (n)	/ˈsʌnʃaɪn/
sure (adj)	/ʃʊə/
swimming (n)	/ˈswɪmɪŋ/
take (v)	/teɪk/
take a photo(graph)	/teɪk ə ˈfəʊtə(grɑːf)/
talk (v)	/tɔːk/
tea (n)	/tiː/
teach (v)	/tiːtʃ/
teacher (n)	/ˈtiːtʃə/
tell (v)	/tel/
thief (n) (TS)	/θiːf/
thing (n)	/θɪŋ/
think (v)	/θɪŋk/
ticket (n)	/ˈtɪkɪt/
tour guide (n)	/ˈtʊə gaɪd/
tourist (n)	/ˈtʊərɪst/
train (n)	/treɪn/
truth (n)	/truːθ/
try (v)	/traɪ/
TV programme (n)	/tiː ˈviː prəʊgræm/
video (n)	/ˈvɪdiəʊ/
visit (v)	/ˈvɪzɪt/
waiter (n)	/ˈweɪtə/

119

WORD LIST

want (v)	/wɒnt/
watch (v)	/wɒtʃ/
wear (v)	/weə/
website (n)	/ˈwebsaɪt/
Welcome to … (TS)	/ˈwelkəm tə/
What about …?	/wɒt əˈbaʊt/
Whose?	/huːz/
Why not?	/waɪ ˈnɒt/
win (v)	/wɪn/
winner (n)	/ˈwɪnə/
woman (pl women) (n)	/ˈwʊmən/ (/ˈwɪmɪn/)
word (n)	/wɜːd/
write (v)	/raɪt/

CLOTHES and ACCESSORIES

badge (n)	/bædʒ/
bag (n)	/bæg/
bangle (n)	/ˈbæŋgəl/
baseball cap (n)	/ˈbeɪsbɔːl kæp/
briefcase (n)	/ˈbriːfkeɪs/
camera (n)	/ˈkæmrə/
fleece (n)	/fliːs/
glasses (n pl)	/ˈglɑːsɪz/
hat (n)	/hæt/
jacket (n)	/ˈdʒækɪt/
jeans (n pl)	/dʒiːnz/
pullover (n)	/ˈpʊləʊvə/
purse (n)	/pɜːs/
scarf (n)	/skɑːf/
shirt (n)	/ʃɜːt/
shoe (n)	/ʃuː/
shorts (n)	/ʃɔːts/
sunglasses (n pl)	/ˈsʌnglɑːsɪz/
sweatshirt (n)	/ˈswetʃɜːt/
T-shirt (n)	/ˈtiːʃɜːt/
top (n)	/tɒp/
trainer (n)	/ˈtreɪnə/
trousers (n pl)	/ˈtraʊzəz/
umbrella (n)	/ʌmˈbrelə/
watch (n)	/wɒtʃ/

JOBS IN TELEVISION

actor (n)	/ˈæktə/
cameraman (n)	/ˈkæmrəmæn/
director (n)	/dɪˈrektə, daɪˈrektə/
presenter (n)	/prɪˈzentə/
producer (n)	/prəˈdjuːsə/
scriptwriter (n)	/ˈskrɪptraɪtə/
stuntman (n)	/ˈstʌntmæn/
stuntwoman (n)	/ˈstʌntwʊmən/

CULTURE Welcome to London

also (adv)	/ˈɔːlsəʊ/
bell (n)	/bel/
big (adj)	/bɪg/
big wheel (n)	/ˌbɪg ˈwiːl/
boat (n)	/bəʊt/
canal (n)	/kəˈnæl/
capsule (n)	/ˈkæpsjuːl/
careful (adj)	/ˈkeəfəl/
centre (n)	/ˈsentə/
Christmas Day (n)	/ˌkrɪsməs ˈdeɪ/
city (n)	/ˈsɪti/
climb (v)	/klaɪm/
clock (n)	/klɒk/
column (n)	/ˈkɒləm/
double-decker bus (n)	/ˌdʌbl dekə ˈbʌs/
equal to	/ˈiːkwəl tə/
exact (adj)	/ɪgˈzækt/
exactly (adv)	/ɪgˈzæktli/
exciting (adj)	/ɪkˈsaɪtɪŋ/
face to face	/ˌfeɪs tə ˈfeɪs/
famous (adj)	/ˈfeɪməs/
film character (n)	/ˈfɪlm kærɪktə/
film star (n)	/ˈfɪlm stɑː/

fire (n)	/faɪə/
fruit (n)	/fruːt/
fun (n)	/fʌn/
high (adj)	/haɪ/
history (n)	/ˈhɪstəri/
in fact	/ɪn ˈfækt/
interesting (adj)	/ˈɪntrəstɪŋ/
king (n)	/kɪŋ/
look down	/lʊk ˈdaʊn/
look out	/lʊk ˈaʊt/
metre (m) (n)	/ˈmiːtə/
miss (miss the train) (v)	/mɪs/
model (n)	/ˈmɒdl/
new (adj)	/njuː/
next (adj)	/nekst/
open (adj)	/ˈəʊpn/
own (adj)	/əʊn/
past (prep)	/pɑːst/
place (n)	/pleɪs/
popular (adj)	/ˈpɒpjələ/
queen (n)	/kwiːn/
real (adj)	/riːl/
rebuild (v)	/riːˈbɪld/
record (n)	/ˈrekɔːd/
ride (n & v)	/raɪd/
salt (n)	/sɒlt/
seawater (n)	/ˈsiːwɔːtə/
shark (n)	/ʃɑːk/
shopping (n)	/ˈʃɒpɪŋ/
site (n)	/saɪt/
sky (n)	/skaɪ/
slow (adj)	/sləʊ/
start (v)	/stɑːt/
stone (adj)	/stəʊn/
street theatre (n)	/ˈstriːt θɪətə/
tall (adj)	/tɔːl/
taxi (n)	/ˈtæksi/
tonne (n)	/tʌn/
tour (n)	/tʊə/
tourist attraction (n)	/ˈtʊərɪst əˌtrækʃən/
travel (v)	/ˈtrævəl/
unusual (adj)	/ʌnˈjuːʒuəl/
vegetable (n)	/ˈvedʒtəbəl/
view (n)	/vjuː/
weekend (n)	/ˌwiːkˈend/
weigh (v)	/weɪ/
weight (n)	/weɪt/
whisper (v)	/ˈwɪspə/
world (n)	/wɜːld/

PLACES IN A TOWN

aquarium (n)	/əˈkweəriəm/
café (n)	/ˈkæfeɪ/
cathedral (n)	/kəˈθiːdrəl/
church (n)	/tʃɜːtʃ/
clock tower (n)	/ˈklɒk taʊə/
market (n)	/ˈmɑːkɪt/
monument (n)	/ˈmɒnjʊmənt/
museum (n)	/mjuːˈziəm/
park (n)	/pɑːk/
restaurant (n)	/ˈrestrɒnt/
zoo (n)	/zuː/

Unit 2

address (n)	/əˈdres/
age (n)	/eɪdʒ/
agree (with) (v)	/əˈgriː (wɪð)/
all-night (adj)	/ˈɔːl naɪt/
amazing (adj)	/əˈmeɪzɪŋ/
answer (v)	/ˈɑːnsə/
anything (pron)	/ˈeniθɪŋ/
arrival (n)	/əˈraɪvəl/
arrive (v)	/əˈraɪv/

ask (v)	/ɑːsk/
bad at	/ˈbæd æt/
ball (n)	/bɔːl/
band (n)	/bænd/
beach (n)	/biːtʃ/
book (v)	/bʊk/
bossy (adj)	/ˈbɒsi/
bottle (n)	/ˈbɒtəl/
bread (n)	/bred/
bring (v)	/brɪŋ/
burn (v)	/bɜːn/
Bye.	/baɪ/
candle (n)	/ˈkændəl/
can't stand	/kɑːnt ˈstænd/
carnival (n)	/ˈkɑːnɪvəl/
carry (v)	/ˈkæri/
celebrate (v)	/ˈseləbreɪt/
celebration (n)	/seləˈbreɪʃən/
champagne (n)	/ʃæmˈpeɪn/
change (money) (v)	/tʃeɪndʒ (mʌni)/
cheek (n)	/tʃiːk/
child (pl children) (n)	/tʃaɪld/ (/ˈtʃɪldrən/)
choose (v)	/tʃuːz/
cigarette (n)	/ˈsɪgəret/
cold (adj)	/kəʊld/
colourful (adj)	/ˈkʌləfəl/
come back	/kʌm ˈbæk/
cosmopolitan (adj)	/kɒzməˈpɒlɪtən/
cost (v)	/kɒst/
costume (n)	/ˈkɒstʃuːm/
crowd (n)	/kraʊd/
country (n)	/ˈkʌntri/
cup (n)	/kʌp/
dance (v)	/dɑːns/
dancer (n)	/ˈdɑːnsə/
direction (n)	/dɪˈrekʃən, daɪˈrekʃən/
dragon (n)	/ˈdrægən/
drink (v)	/drɪŋk/
drummer (n)	/ˈdrʌmə/
dry (adj)	/draɪ/
early (adv)	/ˈɜːli/
at the end of	/ət ðiː ˈend əv/
eat (v)	/iːt/
enjoy (v)	/ɪnˈdʒɔɪ/
envelope (n)	/ˈenvələʊp/
even (adv)	/ˈiːvən/
everything (pron)	/ˈevriθɪŋ/
exotic (adj)	/ɪgˈzɒtɪk/
fantastic (adj)	/fænˈtæstɪk/
festival (n)	/ˈfestɪvəl/
find (v)	/faɪnd/
fireworks (n pl)	/ˈfaɪəwɜːks/
first (adv)	/fɜːst/
flight (n)	/flaɪt/
fly (v) (TS)	/flaɪ/
follow (v)	/ˈfɒləʊ/
foreign (adj)	/ˈfɒrɪn/
forget (v)	/fəˈget/
full (of) (adj)	/fʊl (əv)/
game (n)	/geɪm/
get (v)	/get/
1 = become	
2 = receive	
get up	/get ˈʌp/
giant (adj)	/ˈdʒaɪənt/
give (v)	/gɪv/
go away	/gəʊ əˈweɪ/
go on	/gəʊ ˈɒn/
good at	/gʊd æt/
good luck	/gʊd ˈlʌk/
grape (n)	/greɪp/
greetings card (n)	/ˈgriːtɪŋz kɑːd/
guest (n)	/gest/
haircut (n)	/ˈheəkʌt/
hate (v)	/heɪt/
home (n)	/həʊm/
homework (n)	/ˈhəʊmwɜːk/
house (n)	/haʊs/
How long?	/haʊ ˈlɒŋ/

WORD LIST

How many?	/haʊ ˈmeni/
hungry (adj)	/ˈhʌŋgri/
immediately (adv)	/ɪˈmiːdiətli/
including (prep)	/ɪŋkluːdɪŋ/
interested (adj)	/ˈɪntrəstɪd/
interview (v)	/ˈɪntəvjuː/
into (prep)	/ˈɪntə/
jewellery (n)	/ˈdʒuːəlri/
judge (n)	/dʒʌdʒ/
jump (n)	/dʒʌmp/
kind (What kind?) (n)	/kaɪnd/
kiss (v)	/kɪs/
large (adj)	/lɑːdʒ/
last (v)	/lɑːst/
lentils (n pl)	/ˈlentəlz/
letter (write a letter) (n)	/ˈletə/
light (n)	/laɪt/
lion (n)	/ˈlaɪən/
long (adj)	/lɒŋ/
look after	/lʊk ˈɑːftə/
look for	/lʊk fə/
lose (v)	/luːz/
lost (adj)	/lɒst/
loud (adj)	/laʊd/
make a wish	/meɪk ə ˈwɪʃ/
meal (n)	/miːl/
medicine (n)	/ˈmedsən/
member (n)	/ˈmembə/
money (n)	/ˈmʌni/
New Year	/njuː ˈjɪə/
New Year's Eve	/ˌnjuː jɪəz ˈiːv/
nice (adj)	/naɪs/
noisy (adj)	/ˈnɔɪzi/
non-stop (adj)	/ˈnɒn stɒp/
noodles (n pl)	/ˈnuːdəlz/
notice (v)	/ˈnəʊtɪs/
old (adj)	/əʊld/
once (adv)	/wʌns/
on your own	/ɒn jɔː(r) ˈəʊn/
once (adv)	/wʌns/
open (v)	/ˈəʊpn/
parade (n & v)	/pəˈreɪd/
party (n)	/ˈpɑːti/
perform (v)	/pəˈfɔːm/
plate (n)	/pleɪt/
poem (n)	/ˈpəʊɪm/
police (n)	/pəˈliːs/
present (n)	/ˈpreznt/
questionnaire (n)	/kwestʃəˈneə/
quiet (adj)	/ˈkwaɪət/
radio (n) (TS)	/ˈreɪdiəʊ/
region (n)	/ˈriːdʒən/
rest (= others) (n)	/rest/
rice (n)	/raɪs/
ring (v)	/rɪŋ/
rude (adj)	/ruːd/
safe (adj)	/seɪf/
samba (n)	/ˈsæmbə/
same (adj)	/seɪm/
say (v)	/seɪ/
secret (n) (TS)	/ˈsiːkrət/
send (v)	/send/
shake hands	/ʃeɪk ˈhændz/
show (n)	/ʃəʊ/
should (v)	/ʃʊd/
sign (n)	/saɪn/
sing (v)	/sɪŋ/
size (n)	/saɪz/
small (adj)	/smɔːl/
smart (adj)	/smɑːt/
song (n)	/sɒŋ/
sound system (n)	/ˈsaʊnd sɪstəm/
soup (n)	/suːp/
spectacular (adj)	/spekˈtækjʊlə/
stage (n)	/steɪdʒ/
stall (n)	/stɔːl/
stamp (n)	/stæmp/
start (n)	/stɑːt/
street (n)	/striːt/
street party (n)	/striːt pɑːti/
stupid (adj)	/ˈstjuːpɪd/
suitcase (n)	/ˈsuːtkeɪs/
team (n)	/tiːm/
telephone (n)	/ˈtelɪfəʊn/
Thailand	/ˈtaɪlænd/
thank you	/θæŋk juː/
throw (v)	/θrəʊ/
together (adv)	/təˈgeðə/
tradition (n)	/trəˈdɪʃən/
traditional (adj)	/trəˈdɪʃnəl/
twice (adv)	/twaɪs/
underwear (n)	/ˈʌndəweə/
until (conj)	/ənˈtɪl/
use (v) (TS)	/juːz/
Venezuela	/venəzˈweɪlə/
visitor (n)	/ˈvɪzɪtə/
wait (for) (v)	/weɪt/
walk (v)	/wɔːk/
warm (adj)	/wɔːm/
water (n)	/ˈwɔːtə/
wave (n)	/weɪv/
weather (n)	/ˈweðə/
well-known (adj)	/wel nəʊn/
wet (adj)	/wet/
window (n)	/ˈwɪndəʊ/
wine (n)	/waɪn/

MUSIC

heavy metal	/hevi ˈmetəl/
house	/haʊs/
jazz	/dʒæz/
pop	/pɒp/
punk	/pʌŋk/
rap	/ræp/
reggae	/ˈregeɪ/
rock	/rɒk/
soul	/səʊl/
techno	/ˈteknəʊ/
world	/wɜːld/

PREPOSITIONS OF PLACE

behind	/bɪˈhaɪnd/
between	/bɪˈtwiːn/
in front of	/ɪn ˈfrʌnt əv/
inside	/ɪnˈsaɪd/
near	/nɪə/
next to	/neks tə/
opposite	/ˈɒpəzɪt/
outside	/aʊtˈsaɪd/
over	/ˈəʊvə/
under	/ˈʌndə/

TOWN FACILITIES

bank (n)	/bæŋk/
bookshop (n)	/ˈbʊkʃɒp/
chemist's (n)	/ˈkemɪsts/
flower shop (n)	/ˈflaʊə ʃɒp/
hairdresser's (n)	/ˈheədresəz/
newsagent's (n)	/ˈnjuːzeɪdʒənts/
police station (n)	/pəˈliːs steɪʃən/
post office (n)	/ˈpəʊst ɒfɪs/
stadium (n)	/ˈsteɪdiəm/
supermarket (n)	/ˈsuːpəmɑːkɪt/
travel agency (n)	/ˈtrævəl eɪdʒənsi/

REVIEW UNITS 1–2

bonfire (n)	/ˈbɒnfaɪə/
carriage (n)	/ˈkærɪdʒ/
central (adj)	/ˈsentrəl/
Christmas tree (n)	/ˈkrɪsməs triː/
Easter (n)	/ˈiːstə/
enough (adj)	/ɪˈnʌf/
failure (n)	/ˈfeɪljə/
lift (in a car) (n)	/lɪft/
Hindu (n & adj)	/ˈhɪnduː/
mobile (phone) (n)	/ˈməʊbaɪl/
phone card (n)	/ˈfəʊn kɑːd/
public (adj)	/ˈpʌblɪk/
show (v)	/ʃəʊ/
stranger (n)	/ˈstreɪndʒə/

Unit 3

asleep (adj)	/əˈsliːp/
at first (adv)	/ət ˈfɜːst/
ball-point pen (n)	/ˈbɔːl pɔɪnt ˈpen/
beautiful (adj)	/ˈbjuːtɪfəl/
become (v)	/bɪˈkʌm/
bestseller (n)	/ˈbestselə/
be born (v)	/biː ˈbɔːn/
brilliant (adj)	/ˈbrɪljənt/
brandy (n)	/ˈbrændi/
bridge (n)	/brɪdʒ/
build (v)	/bɪld/
building (n)	/ˈbɪldɪŋ/
burn (down) (v)	/bɜːn (ˈdaʊn)/
bury (v)	/ˈberi/
butter (n)	/ˈbʌtə/
call (v)	/kɔːl/
career (n)	/kəˈrɪə/
cassette (n)	/kəˈset/
cassette recorder (n)	/kəˈset rɪˌkɔːdə/
century (n)	/ˈsentʃʊri/
cheese (n)	/tʃiːz/
close (adj)	/kləʊs/
coast (n)	/kəʊst/
collect (v)	/kəˈlekt/
come down	/kʌm ˈdaʊn/
complete (adj)	/kəmˈpliːt/
cross (v)	/krɒs/
cruise (n)	/kruːz/
cry (v)	/kraɪ/
death (n)	/deθ/
decide (v)	/dɪˈsaɪd/
describe (v)	/dɪsˈkraɪb/
design (v)	/dɪˈzaɪn/
destroy (v)	/dɪsˈtrɔɪ/
diary (n)	/ˈdaɪəri/
die (v)	/daɪ/
emergency (adj)	/ɪˈmɜːdʒənsi/
escape (n & v)	/ɪsˈkeɪp/
event (n)	/ɪˈvent/
eye (n)	/aɪ/
exhausted (adj)	/ɪgˈzɔːstɪd/
exhibition (n)	/eksɪˈbɪʃən/
extremely (adv)	/ɪkˈstriːmli/
factory (n)	/ˈfæktri/
fall (v)	/fɔːl/
fame (n)	/feɪm/
feel (v)	/fiːl/
field (n)	/fiːld/
flame (n)	/fleɪm/
fortune (n)	/ˈfɔːtʃuːn/
funny (adj)	/ˈfʌni/
gallery (n)	/ˈgæləri/
ghost story (n)	/ˈgəʊst stɔːri/
guys (n pl)	/gaɪz/
have fun	/hæv ˈfʌn/
hit (v)	/hɪt/
hot (adj)	/hɒt/
hurt (v)	/hɜːt/
ice cream (n)	/ˈaɪs kriːm/
idea (n)	/aɪˈdɪə/
impossible (adj)	/ɪmˈpɒsɪbəl/
inflammable (adj)	/ɪnˈflæməbəl/
invent (v)	/ɪnˈvent/
join (v)	/dʒɔɪn/
laugh (v)	/lɑːf/

WORD LIST

lazy (adj)	/ˈleɪzi/
life (n)	/laɪf/
lifebelt (n)	/ˈlaɪfbelt/
lucky (adj)	/ˈlʌki/
lunch (n)	/lʌntʃ/
major (adj)	/ˈmeɪdʒə/
make a phone call	/ˌmeɪk ə ˈfəʊn kɔːl/
marry (v)	/ˈmæri/
move (to) (v)	/muːv (tə)/
nearly (adv)	/ˈnɪəli/
newspaper (n)	/ˈnjuːspeɪpə/
nightclothes (n pl)	/ˈnaɪtkləʊðz/
novel (n)	/ˈnɒvəl/
oil (n)	/ɔɪl/
on fire	/ɒn ˈfaɪə/
overboard (adv)	/əʊvəˈbɔːd/
Ow!	/aʊ/
pack (v)	/pæk/
part-owner (n)	/ˌpɑːt ˈəʊnə/
pass (v)	/pɑːs/
payment (n)	/ˈpeɪmənt/
phone call (n)	/ˈfəʊn kɔːl/
picnic (n)	/ˈpɪknɪk/
point (v)	/pɔɪnt/
present (adj)	/ˈprezənt/
print (v)	/prɪnt/
probably (adv)	/ˈprɒbəbli/
publish (v)	/ˈpʌblɪʃ/
pull (v)	/pʊl/
quiz (n)	/kwɪz/
rain (n & v)	/reɪn/
reach (v)	/riːtʃ/
receive (v)	/rɪˈsiːv/
record (v)	/rɪˈkɔːd/
record shop (n)	/ˈrekɔːd ʃɒp/
rescue (v)	/ˈreskjuː/
return (v)	/rɪˈtɜːn/
rich (adj)	/rɪtʃ/
rock (n)	/rɒk/
rubbish (n)	/ˈrʌbɪʃ/
sail (v)	/seɪl/
school (n)	/skuːl/
sea (n)	/siː/
several (adj)	/ˈsevrəl/
shine (v)	/ʃaɪn/
shiver (v)	/ˈʃɪvə/
show (v)	/ʃəʊ/
silly (adj)	/ˈsɪli/
sink (v) (TS)	/sɪŋk/
smile (v)	/smaɪl/
smoke (n)	/sməʊk/
space (n)	/speɪs/
spend (time) (v)	/spend (ˈtaɪm)/
step (n)	/step/
storm (n)	/stɔːm/
story (n)	/ˈstɔːri/
study (v)	/ˈstʌdi/
success (n)	/səkˈses/
successful (adj) (TS)	/səkˈsesfəl/
suddenly (adv)	/ˈsʌdənli/
sun (n)	/sʌn/
surf (the Internet) (v)	/sɜːf (ði: ˈɪntənet)/
take a picture	/teɪk ə ˈpɪktʃə/
terrible (adj)	/ˈterɪbəl/
terrific (adj)	/təˈrɪfɪk/
Thank goodness!	/θæŋk ˈgʊdnəs/
thatched roof (n)	/ˈθætʃt ruːf/
thirsty (adj)	/ˈθɜːsti/
tired (adj)	/ˈtaɪəd/
top (n)	/tɒp/
typewriter (n)	/ˈtaɪpraɪtə/
university (n)	/juːnɪˈvɜːsɪti/
Walkman (n)	/ˈwɔːkmən/
well-known (adj)	/ˌwel ˈnəʊn/
What on earth …?	/wɒt ɒn ˈɜːθ/
whale (n)	/weɪl/
whistle (v)	/ˈwɪsəl/
wind (n)	/wɪnd/
wonderful (adj)	/ˈwʌndəfəl/
work (n & v)	/wɜːk/

JOBS and OCCUPATIONS (1)

architect (n)	/ˈɑːkɪtekt/
artist (n)	/ˈɑːtɪst/
baker (n)	/ˈbeɪkə/
novelist (n)	/ˈnɒvəlɪst/
playwright (n)	/ˈpleɪraɪt/
politician (n)	/ˌpɒlɪˈtɪʃən/
scientist (n)	/ˈsaɪəntɪst/
teacher (n)	/ˈtiːtʃə/
writer (n)	/ˈraɪtə/

PLAYS

acting company (n)	/ˈæktɪŋ ˌkʌmpəni/
performance (n)	/pəˈfɔːməns/
play (n)	/pleɪ/
theatre (n)	/ˈθɪətə/
tragedy (n)	/ˈtrædʒədi/

TIME REFERENCE WORDS

after (prep)	/ˈɑːftə/
ago (prep)	/əˈgəʊ/
between (prep)	/bɪˈtwiːn/
by (prep)	/baɪ/
finally (adv)	/ˈfaɪnəli/
for (prep)	/fɔː/
in (prep)	/ɪn/
later (adv)	/ˈleɪtə/
next (adj)	/nekst/
on (prep)	/ɒn/
soon (adv)	/suːn/
still (adv)	/stɪl/
then (adv)	/ðen/
until (conj & prep)	/ənˈtɪl/
when (conj)	/wen/

TRANSPORT (1)

bicycle (n)	/ˈbaɪsɪkəl/
big wheel (n)	/ˌbɪg ˈwiːl/
boat (n)	/bəʊt/
bus (n)	/bʌs/
car (n)	/kɑː/
helicopter (n)	/ˈhelɪkɒptə/
plane (n)	/pleɪn/
rocket (n)	/ˈrɒkɪt/
ship (n)	/ʃɪp/
spaceship (n)	/ˈspeɪsʃɪp/
speedboat (n)	/ˈspiːdbəʊt/
taxi (n)	/ˈtæksi/
train (n)	/treɪn/

CULTURE Hello New York!

apartment (n) (AmE)	/əˈpɑːtmənt/
area (n)	/ˈeəriə/
biscuit (n)	/ˈbɪskɪt/
car park (n)	/ˈkɑː pɑːk/
cell phone (n) (AmE)	/ˈsel fəʊn/
chips (n pl)	/tʃɪps/
covered with	/ˈkʌvəd wɪð/
discover (v)	/dɪsˈkʌvə/
drugstore (n) (AmE)	/ˈdrʌgstɔː/
Dutch (adj & n)	/dʌtʃ/
explorer (n)	/ɪkˈsplɔːrə/
flat (n)	/flæt/
forest (n)	/ˈfɒrɪst/
French fries (n pl) (AmE)	/ˌfrentʃ ˈfraɪz/
garbage (n) (AmE)	/ˈgɑːbɪdʒ/
grammar (n)	/ˈgræmə/
harbour (n)	/ˈhɑːbə/
island (n)	/ˈaɪlənd/
Native American (n)	/ˌneɪtɪv əˈmerɪkən/
nonsense (n)	/ˈnɒnsəns/
pants (n pl) (AmE)	/pænts/
parking lot (n) (AmE)	/ˈpɑːkɪŋ lɒt/
piece (n)	/piːs/
railroad (n) (AmE)	/ˈreɪlrəʊd/
railway (n)	/ˈreɪlweɪ/
sneakers (n pl) (AmE)	/ˈsniːkəz/
store (n) (AmE)	/stɔː/
trash (n) (AmE)	/træʃ/
vocabulary (n)	/vəʊˈkæbjʊləri/

Unit 4

a bit (adv)	/ə ˈbɪt/
absurd (adj)	/əbˈzɜːd/
accident (n)	/ˈæksɪdənt/
act (v)	/ækt/
action (n)	/ˈækʃən/
action-packed (adj)	/ˈækʃənpækt/
activity (n)	/ækˈtɪvɪti/
afraid (adj)	/əˈfreɪd/
I'm afraid (= I'm sorry)	/aɪm əˈfreɪd/
anyone (pron)	/ˈeniwʌn/
appear (v)	/əˈpɪə/
backwards (adv)	/ˈbækwədz/
Best wishes.	/best ˈwɪʃɪz/
boring (adj)	/ˈbɔːrɪŋ/
camp (v)	/kæmp/
camping site (n)	/ˈkæmpɪŋ saɪt/
caravan (n)	/ˈkærəvæn/
card (n) (TS)	/kɑːd/
cat (n)	/kæt/
chair (n)	/tʃeə/
cheap (adj)	/tʃiːp/
clear (adj) (TS)	/klɪə/
comfortable (adj)	/ˈkʌmftəbəl/
copy (v)	/ˈkɒpi/
crash (v) (TS)	/kræʃ/
crazy (adj)	/ˈkreɪzi/
curtain (n)	/ˈkɜːtən/
drama exercise (n)	/ˈdrɑːmə(r) eksəsaɪz/
drum (n)	/drʌm/
doctor (n)	/ˈdɒktə/
fast (adj)	/fɑːst/
fast-moving (adj)	/ˈfɑːst muːvɪŋ/
free (from prison) (adj)	/friː/
future (n)	/ˈfjuːtʃə/
get (= obtain) (v)	/get/
get on (well)	/get ˈɒn/
have a go	/hæv ə ˈgəʊ/
gossip (n)	/ˈgɒsɪp/
gun (n)	/gʌn/
hard (adj & adv)	/hɑːd/
have an argument	/hæv ən ˈɑːgjəmənt/
hospital (n)	/ˈhɒspɪtəl/
illness (n)	/ˈɪlnəs/
imaginary (adj)	/ɪˈmædʒɪnri/
keep in touch	/ˌkiːp ɪn ˈtʌtʃ/
kill (v)	/kɪl/
knock over (TS)	/ˌnɒk ˈəʊvə/
local (adj)	/ˈləʊkəl/
manager (n)	/ˈmænɪdʒə/
manner (n)	/ˈmænə/
move over	/muːv ˈəʊvə/
murderer (n)	/ˈmɜːdərə/
need (v)	/niːd/
nervous (adj)	/ˈnɜːvəs/
news (bad news) (n)	/njuːz/
normally (adv)	/ˈnɔːməli/
nurse (n)	/nɜːs/
ourselves (pron)	/aʊˈselvz/
patient (n)	/ˈpeɪʃnt/
plan (n)	/plæn/

WORD LIST

pleased (adj)	/pliːzd/
pool (game) (n)	/puːl/
practise (v)	/præktɪs/
prefer (v)	/prɪˈfɜː/
prison (n)	/prɪzn/
pub (n)	/pʌb/
ready (adj)	/redi/
recent (adj)	/riːsənt/
relationship (n)	/rɪˈleɪʃənʃɪp/
reply (v) (TS)	/rɪˈplaɪ/
revenge (n)	/rɪˈvendʒ/
robbery (n)	/rɒbəri/
romance (n)	/rəʊˈmæns/
rope (n)	/rəʊp/
sad (adj)	/sæd/
seem (v)	/siːm/
serious (adj)	/sɪəriəs/
setting (n)	/setɪŋ/
Sh!	/ʃ/
What a shame!	/wɒt ə ˈʃeɪm/
shoot (v)	/ʃuːt/
silence (n)	/saɪləns/
singer (n)	/sɪŋə/
sound (v) (TS)	/saʊnd/
student (n)	/stjuːdənt/
surf (v)	/sɜːf/
surprise (n)	/səˈpraɪz/
surprised (adj)	/səˈpraɪzd/
swim (v)	/swɪm/
take place	/teɪk ˈpleɪs/
telephone (v)	/telɪfəʊn/
terribly (adv)	/terɪbli/
theft (n)	/θeft/
tie up	/taɪ ˈʌp/
treat (v)	/triːt/
trouble (n)	/trʌbəl/
understand (v)	/ʌndəˈstænd/
valuable (adj)	/væljʊbəl/
village (n)	/vɪlɪdʒ/
voice (n) (TS)	/vɔɪs/
walk (n)	/wɔːk/
well (adj)	/wel/
worry (v)	/wʌri/

ADVERBS OF MANNER

angrily	/æŋɡrɪli/
badly	/bædli/
bossily	/bɒsɪli/
carefully	/keəfəli/
comfortably	/kʌmftəbli/
early	/ɜːli/
easily	/iːzɪli/
fast	/fɑːst/
happily	/hæpɪli/
hard	/hɑːd/
hungrily	/hʌŋɡrɪli/
late	/leɪt/
loudly	/laʊdli/
nervously	/nɜːvəsli/
politely	/pəˈlaɪtli/
properly	/prɒpəli/
quickly	/kwɪkli/
quietly	/kwaɪətli/
rudely	/ruːdli/
sadly	/sædli/
slowly	/sləʊli/
thirstily	/θɜːstɪli/
well	/wel/

GRAMMAR WORDS

adjective	/ædʒektɪv/
adverb	/ædvɜːb/
gerund	/dʒerənd/
infinitive	/ɪnˈfɪnɪtɪv/
noun	/naʊn/
preposition	/prepəˈzɪʃən/
pronoun	/prəʊnaʊn/
verb	/vɜːb/

MAKING A TV PROGRAMME

broadcast (n & v)	/brɔːdkɑːst/
cast (n)	/kɑːst/
character (n)	/kærɪktə/
episode (n)	/epɪsəʊd/
microphone (n)	/maɪkrəfəʊn/
performer (n)	/pəˈfɔːmə/
recording (n)	/rɪˈkɔːdɪŋ/
rehearsal (n)	/rɪˈhɜːsəl/
rehearse (v)	/rɪˈhɜːs/
series (n)	/sɪəriːz/
studio (n)	/stjuːdiəʊ/

TV PROGRAMMES

cartoon (n)	/kɑːˈtuːn/
chat show (n)	/tʃæt ʃəʊ/
documentary (n)	/dɒkjəˈmentəri/
drama (n)	/drɑːmə/
game show (n)	/ɡeɪm ʃəʊ/
music programme (n)	/mjuːzɪk ˌprəʊɡræm/
news programme (n)	/njuːz ˌprəʊɡræm/
soap (opera) (n)	/səʊp ˌɒprə/
sports programme (n)	/spɔːts ˌprəʊɡræm/
thriller (n)	/θrɪlə/

REVIEW UNITS 3–4

accept (v)	/əkˈsept/
beautifully (adv)	/bjuːtɪfli/
busy (adj)	/bɪzi/
close (v)	/kləʊz/
explain (v)	/ɪkˈspleɪn/
film (v)	/fɪlm/
promise (v)	/prɒmɪs/
time difference (n)	/taɪm dɪfrəns/
trip (n)	/trɪp/
work out	/wɜːk ˈaʊt/
worried (adj)	/wʌrɪd/

Unit 5

absorb (v)	/əbˈzɔːb/
alternative (n)	/ɔːlˈtɜːnətɪv/
annoying (adj)	/əˈnɔɪɪŋ/
arrangement (n)	/əˈreɪndʒmənt/
backpacker (n)	/bækpækə/
backpacking (n)	/bækpækɪŋ/
borrow (v)	/bɒrəʊ/
cardboard box (n)	/kɑːdbɔːd ˈbɒks/
certainly (adv)	/sɜːtənli/
change (n)	/tʃeɪndʒ/
cheaply (adv)	/tʃiːpli/
closed (adj)	/kləʊzd/
Come on!	/kʌm ˈɒn/
commercial (n)	/kəˈmɜːʃəl/
corner (n)	/kɔːnə/
crowded (adj)	/kraʊdɪd/
customer (n)	/kʌstəmə/
dairy produce (n)	/deəri prɒdjuːs/
department store (n)	/dɪˈpɑːtmənt stɔː/
desert (n) (TS)	/dezət/
dry (v)	/draɪ/
experienced (adj)	/ɪkˈspɪəriənst/
extra (adj)	/ekstrə/
fabulous (adj) (TS)	/fæbjələs/
far (adj)	/fɑː/
fork (n)	/fɔːk/
glass (n)	/ɡlɑːs/
go ahead	/ɡəʊ əˈhed/
heavy (adj)	/hevi/
honestly (adv)	/ɒnəstli/
hopeless (adj)	/həʊpləs/
huge (adj)	/hjuːdʒ/
Hurry up!	/hʌri ˈʌp/
instead (adv)	/ɪnˈsted/
introduction (n)	/ɪntrəˈdʌkʃən/
keep (warm) (v)	/kiːp (ˈwɔːm)/
knife (pl knives)	/naɪf/ (/naɪvz/)
left	/left/
1 on the left (n)	
2 turn left (adv)	
madam	/mædəm/
menu (n)	/menjuː/
miss (= not see) (v)	/mɪs/
natural history (n)	/nætrəl ˈhɪstəri/
New Zealand	/njuː ˈziːlənd/
order (v)	/ɔːdə/
ordinary (adj)	/ɔːdənri/
perfect (adj)	/pɜːfɪkt/
Peru	/pəˈruː/
police officer (n)	/pəˈliːs ɒfɪsə/
postcard (n)	/pəʊskɑːd/
realise (v)	/rɪəlaɪz/
right (turn right) (adv)	/raɪt/
road (n)	/rəʊd/
ruins (n pl) (TS)	/ruːɪnz/
science (n)	/saɪəns/
shoulder (n)	/ʃəʊldə/
Singapore	/sɪŋəˈpɔː/
skin (n)	/skɪn/
souvenir (n) (TS)	/suːvəˈnɪə/
spider (n)	/spaɪdə/
starving (adj)	/stɑːvɪŋ/
strap (n)	/stræp/
strong (adj)	/strɒŋ/
stuff (n)	/stʌf/
suggest (v)	/səˈdʒest/
suggestion (n)	/səˈdʒestʃən/
table (n)	/teɪbəl/
third (n)	/θɜːd/
tip (= suggestion) (n)	/tɪp/
travel writer (n)	/trævəl ˌraɪtə/
traveller (n)	/trævlə/
turn round	/tɜːn ˈraʊnd/
underground (n)	/ʌndəɡraʊnd/
vegetarian (n)	/vedʒəˈteəriən/
wash (v)	/wɒʃ/
wave (v)	/weɪv/
wrong (adj)	/rɒŋ/
young (adj)	/jʌŋ/

CLOTHES and MATERIALS

artificial (adj)	/ɑːtɪˈfɪʃəl/
cloth (n)	/klɒθ/
cotton (n)	/kɒtən/
lightweight (adj)	/laɪtweɪt/
material (n)	/məˈtɪəriəl/
polyester (n)	/pɒliˈestə/
raincoat (n)	/reɪnkəʊt/
suit (n)	/suːt/
sweater (n)	/swetə/
swimming trunks (n pl)	/swɪmɪŋ trʌŋks/
thick (adj) (TS)	/θɪk/
tie (n)	/taɪ/
waterproof (adj)	/wɔːtəpruːf/
wool (n)	/wʊl/

DICTIONARY ABBREVIATIONS

abbreviation (abbrev)	/əbriːviˈeɪʃən/
adjective (adj)	/ædʒektɪv/
adverb (adv)	/ædvɜːb/
auxiliary verb (aux)	/ɔːkˈzɪliəri vɜːb/
countable (C)	/kaʊntəbəl/
plural (pl)	/plʊərəl/
singular (sing)	/sɪŋjələ/

123

WORD LIST

somebody (sb) /ˈsʌmbədi/
something (sth) /ˈsʌmθɪŋ/
uncountable (U) /ʌnˈkaʊntəbəl/

FOOD

bread (n) /bred/
cheese (n) /tʃiːz/
(fried) egg (n) /(fraɪd) eg/
garlic (n) /ˈɡɑːlɪk/
ham (n) /hæm/
meat (n) /miːt/
mushroom (n) /ˈmʌʃrʊm/
olive (n) /ˈɒlɪv/
onion (n) /ˈʌnjən/
pepper (n) /ˈpepə/
pineapple (n) /ˈpaɪnæpəl/
pizza (n) /ˈpiːtsə/
soup (n) /suːp/
spinach (n) /ˈspɪnɪdʒ/
steak (n) /steɪk/
tomato (n) /təˈmɑːtəʊ/

LUGGAGE

backpack (n) /ˈbækpæk/
daypack (n) /ˈdeɪpæk/
rucksack (n) /ˈrʌksæk/
suitcase (n) /ˈsuːtkeɪs/
travel sack (n) /ˈtrævəl sæk/

PREPOSITIONS OF DIRECTION

across /əˈkrɒs/
along /əˈlɒŋ/
down /daʊn/
into /ˈɪntə, ˈɪntuː/
past /pɑːst/
round /raʊnd/
through /θruː/
to /tuː, tə/
up /ʌp/

CULTURE Teenage Life

actually (adv) /ˈæktʊəli/
addictive (adj) /əˈdɪktɪv/
advice (n) /ədˈvaɪs/
anywhere (adv) /ˈeniweə/
cool (adj) /kuːl/
definitely (adv) /ˈdefɪnɪtli/
designer clothes (n pl) /dɪˌzaɪnə ˈkləʊðz/
diet (n) /ˈdaɪət/
disco (n) /ˈdɪskəʊ/
exam (n) /ɪɡˈzæm/
guy (n) /ɡaɪ/
kid (n) /kɪd/
loads of … /ˈləʊdz əv/
marriage (n) /ˈmærɪdʒ/
model /ˈmɒdl/
(fashion model) (n)
obsessive (adj) /əbˈsesɪv/
organise (v) /ˈɔːɡənaɪz/
percentage (n) /pəˈsentɪdʒ/
responsibility (n) /rɪsˌpɒnsɪˈbɪləti/
spend (money) (v) /spend/
survey (n) /ˈsɜːveɪ/
teenager (n) /ˈtiːneɪdʒə/
total (adj) /ˈtəʊtəl/
treat (v) /triːt/
trust (v) /trʌst/
unhappy (adj) /ʌnˈhæpi/
upset (adj) /ʌpˈset/

Unit 6

angel (n) /ˈeɪndʒəl/
animal (n) /ˈænɪməl/
annoyed (adj) /əˈnɔɪd/
balloon (n) /bəˈluːn/
border (n) /ˈbɔːdə/
break (v) /breɪk/
channel (n) /ˈtʃænəl/
Cheer up! /tʃɪə(r) ˈʌp/
conversation (n) /kɒnvəˈseɪʃən/
create (v) /kriˈeɪt/
drive (v) /draɪv/
electric (adj) /ɪˈlektrɪk/
email (n) /ˈiːmeɪl/
embarrassed (adj) /ɪmˈbærɪst/
empty (adj) /ˈempti/
excellent (adj) /ˈeksələnt/
farm (n) /fɑːm/
friendly (adj) /ˈfrendli/
go back /ɡəʊ ˈbæk/
goal (n) (TS) /ɡəʊl/
grass (n) /ɡrɑːs/
guidebook (n) /ˈɡaɪdbʊk/
halfway (adv) /hɑːfˈweɪ/
hard (= difficult) (adj) /hɑːd/
have a shower /hæv ə ˈʃaʊə/
hear of /ˈhɪə(r) əv/
horrible (adj) /ˈhɒrɪbəl/
joke (v) /dʒəʊk/
lift (in a building) (n) /lɪft/
in the middle of /ɪn ðə ˈmɪdl əv/
make a noise /meɪk ə ˈnɔɪz/
mountain (n) /ˈmaʊntɪn/
musical (n) /ˈmjuːzɪkəl/
musician (n) /mjuːˈzɪʃən/
open space (n) /ˌəʊpən ˈspeɪs/
painting (n) /ˈpeɪntɪŋ/
passport (n) /ˈpɑːspɔːt/
personal (adj) (TS) /ˈpɜːsənəl/
pillar (n) /ˈpɪlə/
planet (n) /ˈplænɪt/
plastic bag (n) (TS) /ˈplæstɪk ˈbæɡ/
protect (v) /prəˈtekt/
pull someone's leg /pʊl ˈsʌmwʌnz leɡ/
put up (TS) /pʊt ˈʌp/
queue (n) /kjuː/
reason (n) /ˈriːzən/
right-hand (adj) /raɪt ˈhænd/
satellite TV (n) /ˌsætəlaɪt tiː ˈviː/
Sicily /ˈsɪsɪli/
side (n) /saɪd/
sight (n) /saɪt/
simulator (n) /ˈsɪmjʊleɪtə/
slow down (TS) /sləʊ ˈdaʊn/
sound (n) /saʊnd/
species (n) /ˈspiːʃiːz/
statue (n) /ˈstætʃuː/
steep (adj) /stiːp/
table tennis (n) (TS) /ˈteɪbəl tenɪs/
temple (n) /ˈtempəl/
waterfalls (n pl) /ˈwɔːtəfɔːlz/
whatever (pron) (TS) /wɒtˈevə/
the whole of … /ðə ˈhəʊl əv/
wild (adj) /waɪld/
wildlife (n) /ˈwaɪldlaɪf/
wing (n) (TS) /wɪŋ/
world-famous (adj) /wɜːld ˈfeɪməs/
work out (how to …) /ˌwɜːk ˈaʊt/

ANIMALS (1)

bear (n) /beə/
bird (n) /bɜːd/
cow (n) /kaʊ/
deer (n) /dɪə/
duck (n) /dʌk/
giraffe (n) /dʒɪˈrɑːf/
goat (n) /ɡəʊt/
hippo (n) /ˈhɪpəʊ/
horse (n) /hɔːs/
lion (n) /ˈlaɪən/
monkey (n) /ˈmʌŋki/
pig (n) /pɪɡ/
sheep (n) /ʃiːp/
squirrel (n) /ˈskwɪrəl/
tiger (n) /ˈtaɪɡə/

TRANSPORT (2)

airport (n) /ˈeəpɔːt/
bus driver (n) /ˈbʌs ˌdraɪvə/
bus station (n) /ˈbʌs ˌsteɪʃən/
bus stop (n) /ˈbʌs stɒp/
bus ticket (n) /ˈbʌs ˌtɪkɪt/
bus timetable (n) /ˈbʌs ˌtaɪmteɪbəl/
car driver (n) /ˈkɑː ˌdraɪvə/
car engine (n) /ˈkɑː(r) ˌendʒɪn/
car park (n) /ˈkɑː pɑːk/
ferry boat (n) /ˈferi bəʊt/
railway engine (n) /ˈreɪlweɪ ˌendʒɪn/
railway line (n) /ˈreɪlweɪ laɪn/
railway station (n) /ˈreɪlweɪ ˌsteɪʃən/
traffic (n) /ˈtræfɪk/
train driver (n) /ˈtreɪn ˌdraɪvə/
train station (n) /ˈtreɪn ˌsteɪʃən/
train ticket (n) /ˈtreɪn ˌtɪkɪt/
train timetable (n) /ˈtreɪn ˌtaɪmteɪbəl/
tube (n) /tjuːb/

REVIEW UNITS 5–6

audience (n) /ˈɔːdɪəns/
award (n) /əˈwɔːd/
billion (n) /ˈbɪljən/
hit (n) /hɪt/
household name (n) /ˌhaʊshəʊld ˈneɪm/
single (n) /ˈsɪŋɡəl/
worldwide (adj) /ˈwɜːldwaɪd/

Unit 7

absolutely (adv) /ˈæbsəluːtli/
advertisement (n) /ədˈvɜːtɪsmənt/
ages (n pl) /ˈeɪdʒɪz/
alive (adj) /əˈlaɪv/
alone (adv) /əˈləʊn/
amongst (prep) /əˈmʌŋst/
animated display (n) /ˈænɪmeɪtɪd dɪˈspleɪ/
autograph (n) /ˈɔːtəɡrɑːf/
baby (n) /ˈbeɪbi/
bar (n) /bɑː/
basic (adj) /ˈbeɪsɪk/
beans (n pl) /biːnz/
bite (n) /baɪt/
brain (n) /breɪn/
camp (n) /kæmp/
care (v) /keə/
catch (a train/bus) (v) /kætʃ (ə treɪn, bʌs)/
celebrity (n) /səˈlebrɪti/
charity (n) /ˈtʃærɪti/
check-out (n) /ˈtʃekaʊt/
chopping board (n) /ˈtʃɒpɪŋ bɔːd/
clap (v) /klæp/
clean (v) /kliːn/
clearly (adv) /ˈklɪəli/
complain (v) /kəmˈpleɪn/
contact (n) /ˈkɒntækt/
contestant (n) /kənˈtestənt/
cook (v) /kʊk/
cooking pot (n) /ˈkʊkɪŋ pɒt/

WORD LIST

creature (n)	/ˈkriːtʃə/
cross-country skiing (n)	/ˌkrɒs ˌkʌntri ˈskiːɪŋ/
culture (n)	/ˈkʌltʃə/
danger (n)	/ˈdeɪndʒə/
deep (adj)	/diːp/
details (n pl)	/ˈdiːteɪlz/
develop (v)	/dɪˈveləp/
downhill (adv) (TS)	/ˌdaʊnˈhɪl/
during (prep)	/ˈdʒʊərɪŋ/
earthquake (n)	/ˈɜːθkweɪk/
enter (v)	/ˈentə/
environment (n)	/ɪnˈvaɪrənmənt/
equipment (n)	/ɪˈkwɪpmənt/
erupt (v)	/ɪˈrʌpt/
eruption (n)	/ɪˈrʌpʃən/
exhausting (adj)	/ɪkˈzɔːstɪŋ/
experience (v)	/ɪkˈspɪəriəns/
extinct (adj)	/ɪkˈstɪŋkt/
extraordinary (adj)	/ɪkˈstrɔːdənri/
fascinating (adj)	/ˈfæsɪneɪtɪŋ/
feather (n)	/ˈfeðə/
feed (v)	/fiːd/
film crew (n)	/ˈfɪlm kruː/
Finland	/ˈfɪnlənd/
flash (v)	/flæʃ/
flash photograph (n)	/ˈflæʃ ˈfəʊtəɡrɑːf/
fortnight (n)	/ˈfɔːtnaɪt/
fortunately (adv)	/ˈfɔːtʃənətli/
frightening (adj)	/ˈfraɪtnɪŋ/
frown (n)	/fraʊn/
give up	/ɡɪv ˈʌp/
grow (v)	/ɡrəʊ/
hide (v)	/haɪd/
highlight (n)	/ˈhaɪlaɪt/
human being (n)	/ˌhjuːmən ˈbiːɪŋ/
increased (adj)	/ɪnˈkriːst/
inhabitant (n)	/ɪnˈhæbɪtənt/
intelligent (adj)	/ɪnˈtelɪdʒənt/
interact (v)	/ɪntəˈrækt/
interactive (adj)	/ɪntəˈræktɪv/
item (n)	/ˈaɪtəm/
journey (n)	/ˈdʒɜːni/
jungle (n)	/ˈdʒʌŋɡəl/
law (n)	/lɔː/
lay eggs	/leɪ ˈeɡz/
library (n)	/ˈlaɪbrəri/
litter (n)	/ˈlɪtə/
live (adj)	/laɪv/
log (n)	/lɒɡ/
luxury (n)	/ˈlʌkʃəri/
major (adj)	/ˈmeɪdʒə/
make the bed	/ˌmeɪk ðə ˈbed/
make a list	/ˌmeɪk ə ˈlɪst/
make-up (n)	/ˈmeɪk ʌp/
matches (n pl)	/ˈmætʃɪz/
means of transport	/ˌmiːnz əv ˈtrænzpɔːt/
melt (v)	/melt/
mind (n)	/maɪnd/
mirror (n)	/ˈmɪrə/
No entry.	/ˌnəʊ ˈentri/
No way!	/ˌnəʊ ˈweɪ/
office (n)	/ˈɒfɪs/
original (adj)	/əˈrɪdʒənəl/
outside world (n)	/ˌaʊtsaɪd ˈwɜːld/
paraffin (n)	/ˈpærəfɪn/
pass (an exam) (v)	/ˌpɑːs (ən ɪɡˈzæm)/
pay (v)	/peɪ/
poisonous (adj)	/ˈpɔɪzənəs/
power (n)	/ˈpaʊə/
provide (v)	/prəˈvaɪd/
put away	/pʊt əˈweɪ/
queue (v)	/kjuː/
rainforest (n)	/ˈreɪnfɒrɪst/
raise (money) (v)	/reɪz (ˈmʌni)/
rather (I'd rather …) (adv)	/ˈrɑːðə/
reality TV show (n)	/riˈæləti tiː ˈviː ʃəʊ/
replica (n)	/ˈreplɪkə/
roar (v)	/rɔː/
seat belt (n)	/ˈsiːt belt/
sentence (n)	/ˈsentəns/
shampoo (n)	/ʃæmˈpuː/
shocking (adj)	/ˈʃɒkɪŋ/
smoke (v)	/sməʊk/
special effects (n pl)	/ˈspeʃl ɪˈfekts/
spoon (n)	/spuːn/
spring (n)	/sprɪŋ/
stretch (v)	/stretʃ/
stunning (adj)	/ˈstʌnɪŋ/
supplies (n pl)	/səˈplaɪz/
surprising (adj)	/səˈpraɪzɪŋ/
survival technique (n)	/səˈvaɪvəl tekˌniːk/
swimming pool (n)	/ˈswɪmɪŋ puːl/
take-off (n)	/ˈteɪk ɒf/
take part	/teɪk ˈpɑːt/
task (n)	/tɑːsk/
terrifying (adj) (TS)	/ˈterɪfaɪɪŋ/
test (n)	/test/
thrill (n)	/θrɪl/
on time	/ɒn ˈtaɪm/
tiring (adj)	/ˈtaɪərɪŋ/
toilet paper (n)	/ˈtɔɪlət peɪpə/
touch (v)	/tʌtʃ/
tourism (n)	/ˈtʊərɪzm/
tourist centre (n)	/ˈtʊərɪst sentə/
traditionally (adv)	/trəˈdɪʃnəli/
treatment (n)	/ˈtriːtmənt/
uphill (adv) (TS)	/ʌpˈhɪl/
version (n)	/ˈvɜːʃən/
viewer (n)	/ˈvjuːə/
visit (n)	/ˈvɪzɪt/
volcano (n)	/vɒlˈkeɪnəʊ/
water cycle (n)	/ˈwɔːtə saɪkəl/
wedding (n)	/ˈwedɪŋ/
Western (adj)	/ˈwestən/
windy (adj)	/ˈwɪndi/
yourself (pron)	/jɔːˈself/

ANIMALS (2)

amphibian (n)	/æmˈfɪbiən/
crocodile (n)	/ˈkrɒkədaɪl/
dinosaur (n)	/ˈdaɪnəsɔː/
herd (n & v)	/hɜːd/
insect (n)	/ˈɪnsekt/
mammal (n)	/ˈmæməl/
octopus (n) (TS)	/ˈɒktəpəs/
reptile (n)	/ˈreptaɪl/
rhino (n)	/ˈraɪnəʊ/
snake (n)	/sneɪk/
tortoise (n)	/ˈtɔːtɪs/
worm (n)	/wɜːm/

THE ARCTIC

freeze (v) (TS)	/friːz/
freezing (adj)	/ˈfriːzɪŋ/
husky (dog)	/ˈhʌski (dɒɡ)/
ice (n)	/aɪs/
Lapland	/ˈlæplænd/
reindeer (n)	/ˈreɪndɪə/
sled (n)	/sled/
snow (n)	/snəʊ/
snowmobile (n)	/ˈsnəʊməbiːl/
tundra (n)	/ˈtʌndrə/

FEELINGS

amazed (adj)	/əˈmeɪzd/
bored (adj)	/bɔːd/
excited (adj)	/ɪkˈsaɪtɪd/
fascinated (adj)	/ˈfæsɪneɪtɪd/
frightened (adj)	/ˈfraɪtnd/
worried (adj)	/ˈwʌrɪd/

HOUSEWORK

do the ironing	/ˌduː ðiː ˈaɪənɪŋ/
do the shopping	/ˌduː ðə ˈʃɒpɪŋ/
do the washing up	/ˌduː ðə wɒʃɪŋ ˈʌp/
lay the table	/ˌleɪ ðə ˈteɪbəl/
make your bed	/ˌmeɪk jɔː ˈbed/

ROOMS

bathroom (n)	/ˈbɑːθruːm/
bedroom (n)	/ˈbedruːm/
kitchen (n)	/ˈkɪtʃɪn/
sitting room (n)	/ˈsɪtɪŋ ruːm/

CULTURE Do the right thing

adult (n)	/ˈædʌlt/
bacon (n)	/ˈbeɪkən/
bend (n)	/bend/
body language (n)	/ˈbɒdi læŋɡwɪdʒ/
bow (v)	/baʊ/
comment (n)	/ˈkɒment/
common (adj)	/ˈkɒmən/
communicate (v)	/kəˈmjuːnɪkeɪt/
cover (n)	/ˈkʌvə/
date (= arrangement) (n)	/deɪt/
disagree (v)	/ˌdɪsəˈɡriː/
encourage (v)	/ɪnˈkʌrɪdʒ/
facial expression (n)	/ˈfeɪʃl ɪkˌspreʃən/
gesture (n)	/ˈdʒestʃə/
hug (v)	/hʌɡ/
in contrast	/ˌɪn ˈkɒntrɑːst/
interest (n)	/ˈɪntrəst/
invite (v)	/ɪnˈvaɪt/
meanwhile (adv)	/ˈmiːnwaɪl/
position (n)	/pəˈzɪʃən/
respond (v)	/rɪsˈpɒnd/
silent (adj)	/ˈsaɪlənt/
stare (v)	/steə/
superior (n)	/suːˈpɪəriə/
table manners (n)	/ˈteɪbəl mænəz/
take off	/teɪk ˈɒf/
thoughtfully (adv)	/ˈθɔːtfəli/
trust (v)	/trʌst/
unfriendly (adj)	/ʌnˈfrendli/

Unit 8

argue (v)	/ˈɑːɡjuː/
blow (v)	/bləʊ/
bone (n)	/bəʊn/
bring to life	/brɪŋ tə ˈlaɪf/
CD player (n)	/siː ˈdiː pleɪə/
Chile	/ˈtʃɪli/
colour (v)	/ˈkʌlə/
compare (v)	/kəmˈpeə/
contact (v)	/ˈkɒntækt/
depressed (adj)	/dɪˈprest/
down (= depressed) (adj)	/daʊn/
DVD player (n)	/ˌdiː viː ˈdiː pleɪə/
exist (v)	/ɪɡˈzɪst/
feeling (n)	/ˈfiːlɪŋ/
fortune teller (n)	/ˈfɔːtʃuːn ˌtelə/
graded reader (n)	/ˌɡreɪdɪd ˈriːdə/
in detail	/ˌɪn ˈdiːteɪl/
information (n)	/ˌɪnfəˈmeɪʃən/
inventor (n)	/ɪnˈventə/
leaf (pl leaves) (n)	/liːf/ (/liːvz/)
manage to do sth	/ˈmænɪdʒ tə ˈduː sʌmθɪŋ/
mathematics (n)	/ˌmæθəˈmætɪks/
mean (= intend) (v)	/miːn/
measure (v)	/ˈmeʒə/
millimetre (mm) (n)	/ˈmɪlɪmiːtə/

WORD LIST

mix (v)	/mɪks/
moon (n)	/muːn/
offer (v)	/ˈɒfə/
plan (v)	/plæn/
press (v)	/pres/
process (n)	/ˈprəʊses/
referee (n)	/ˌrefəˈriː/
refuse (v)	/rɪˈfjuːz/
revise (v)	/rɪˈvaɪz/
save (v)	/seɪv/
schoolboy (n)	/ˈskuːlbɔɪ/
screen (n)	/skriːn/
set (v)	/set/
shout (v)	/ʃaʊt/
splash (v)	/splæʃ/
square (n)	/skweə/
temper (lose your temper) (n)	/ˈtempə/
text message (n)	/ˈtekst mesɪdʒ/
tiny (adj)	/ˈtaɪni/
toothache (n)	/ˈtuːθeɪk/
video recorder (n)	/ˈvɪdɪəʊ rɪˌkɔːdə/
whistle (n)	/ˈwɪsəl/

ANIMATED FILMS

animate (v) (TS)	/ˈænɪmeɪt/
animation (n)	/ˌænɪˈmeɪʃən/
animator (n)	/ˈænɪmeɪtə/
background (n)	/ˈbækgraʊnd/
brightness (n)	/ˈbraɪtnəs/
designer (n)	/dɪˈzaɪnə/
film-maker (n)	/ˈfɪlmmeɪkə/
model (n)	/ˈmɒdəl/
scan (v)	/skæn/
scanner (n) (TS)	/ˈskænə/
scanning (n) (TS)	/ˈskænɪŋ/
storyboard (n)	/ˈstɔːrɪbɔːd/

DIGITAL CAMERAS

button (n)	/ˈbʌtən/
calculation (n)	/ˌkælkjəˈleɪʃən/
computer chip (n)	/kəmˈpjuːtə tʃɪp/
digital photo (n)	/ˌdɪdʒɪtəl ˈfəʊtəʊ/
filter (n)	/ˈfɪltə/
image (n)	/ˈɪmɪdʒ/
pixel (n)	/ˈpɪksəl/
primary colour (n)	/ˌpraɪməri ˈkʌlə/

JOBS AND OCCUPATIONS (2)

computer expert (n)	/kəmˈpjuːtə(r) ˌekspɜːt/
journalist (n)	/ˈdʒɜːnəlɪst/
musician (n)	/mjuːˈzɪʃən/
pilot (n)	/ˈpaɪlət/
tourist guide (n)	/ˈtʊərɪst gaɪd/

REVIEW UNITS 7–8

add (v)	/æd/
air travel (n)	/ˈeə trævəl/
on average	/ɒn ˈævərɪdʒ/
baggage (n)	/ˈbægɪdʒ/
cheat (v)	/tʃiːt/
check in	/tʃek ˈɪn/
competitor (n)	/kəmˈpetɪtə/
enjoyable (adj)	/ɪnˈdʒɔɪəbəl/
entry form (n)	/ˈentri fɔːm/
fatal (adj)	/ˈfeɪtəl/
fit (adj)	/fɪt/
ground (n)	/graʊnd/
instructions (n pl)	/ɪnˈstrʌkʃənz/
intercontinental (adj)	/ˌɪntəkɒntɪˈnentəl/
packet (n)	/ˈpækɪt/
paint (v)	/peɪnt/
permission (n)	/pəˈmɪʃən/
priority (n)	/praɪˈɒrɪti/
safety (n)	/ˈseɪfti/
scissors (n pl)	/ˈsɪzəz/
security (n)	/sɪˈkjʊərɪti/
sharp (adj)	/ʃɑːp/
sign (v)	/saɪn/
take exercise	/ˌteɪk ˈeksəsaɪz/
warm up	/wɔːm ˈʌp/
X-ray (n)	/ˈeks reɪ/

PRONUNCIATION GUIDE

Vowels

/ɑː/	arm, large
/æ/	cap, bad
/aɪ/	ride, fly
/aɪə/	diary, science
/aʊ/	how, mouth
/aʊə/	our, shower
/e/	bed, head
/eɪ/	day, grey
/eə/	hair, there
/ɪ/	give, did
/i/	happy, taxi
/iː/	we, heat
/ɪə/	ear, here
/ɒ/	not, watch
/əʊ/	cold, boat
/ɔː/	door, talk
/ɔɪ/	point, boy
/ʊ/	foot, could
/uː/	two, food
/ʊə/	sure, tourist
/ɜː/	bird, heard
/ʌ/	fun, come
/ə/	mother, actor

Consonants

/b/	bag, rubbish
/d/	desk, cold
/f/	fill, laugh
/g/	girl, big
/h/	hand, home
/j/	yes, young
/k/	cook, back
/l/	like, fill
/m/	mean, climb
/n/	new, want
/p/	park, happy
/r/	ring, borrow
/s/	say, this
/t/	town, city
/v/	very, live
/w/	water, away
/z/	zoo, his
/ʃ/	shop, machine
/ʒ/	usually, television
/ŋ/	thank, doing
/tʃ/	cheese, picture
/θ/	thing, north
/ð/	that, clothes
/dʒ/	jeans, bridge

IRREGULAR VERBS

Infinitive	Past simple	Past participle
be	was, were	been
become	became	become
begin	began	begun
blow	blew	blown
break	broke	broken
bring	brought	brought
broadcast	broadcast	broadcast
build	built	built
burn	burnt/burned	burnt/burned
buy	bought	bought
catch	caught	caught
choose	chose	chosen
come	came	come
cost	cost	cost
do	did	done
draw	drew	drawn
dream	dreamt/dreamed	dreamt/dreamed
drink	drank	drunk
drive	drove	driven
eat	ate	eaten
fall	fell	fallen
feed	fed	fed
feel	felt	felt
fight	fought	fought
find	found	found
fly	flew	flown
forget	forgot	forgotten
freeze	froze	frozen
get	got	got
give	gave	given
go	went	gone/been
grow	grew	grown
hang	hung	hung
have	had	had
hear	heard	heard
hide	hid	hidden
hit	hit	hit
hold	held	held
hurt	hurt	hurt
keep	kept	kept
know	knew	known
lay	laid	laid
learn	learnt/learned	learnt/learned
leave	left	left

Infinitive	Past simple	Past participle
lend	lent	lent
let	let	let
light	lit	lit
lose	lost	lost
make	made	made
mean	meant	meant
meet	met	met
pay	paid	paid
put	put	put
read /ri:d/	read /red/	read /red/
rebuild	rebuilt	rebuilt
rewrite	rewrote	rewritten
ride	rode	ridden
ring	rang	rung
run	ran	run
say	said	said
see	saw	seen
sell	sold	sold
send	sent	sent
shake	shook	shaken
shine	shone	shone
shoot	shot	shot
show	showed	shown
sing	sang	sung
sink	sank	sunk
sit	sat	sat
sleep	slept	slept
speak	spoke	spoken
spell	spelt/spelled	spelt/spelled
spend	spent	spent
stand	stood	stood
steal	stole	stolen
swim	swam	swum
take	took	taken
teach	taught	taught
tell	told	told
think	thought	thought
throw	threw	thrown
understand	understood	understood
wake	woke	woken
wear	wore	worn
win	won	won
write	wrote	written

Macmillan Education
Between Towns Road, Oxford OX4 3PP
A division of Macmillan Publishers Limited
Companies and representatives throughout the world

ISBN 10: 1-4050-2940-4
ISBN 13: 978-1-4050-2940-7

Text © Judy Garton-Sprenger and Philip Prowse 2005
Design and illustration © Macmillan Publishers Limited 2005

The rights of Judy Garton-Sprenger and Philip Prowse to be identified as authors of this work have been asserted by them in accordance with the Copyright, Designs and Patents Act 1988.

First published 2005

All rights reserved; no part of this publication may be reproduced, stored in a retrieval system, transmitted in any form, or by any means, electronic, mechanical, photocopying, recording, or otherwise, without the prior written permission of the publishers.

Designed by Giles Davies Design
Illustrated by Giles Davies pp23(m), 59(t); Roger Fereday p90;
Clive Goodyer pp23(b), 106(b), 116(b); Neil Gower p59; Julia Pearson pp106(t), 116(t); Kate Sheppard pp16, 40, 64, 88; Nadine Wickenden pp23(t), 37, 81, 83
Cover design by Sue Ayres
Cover illustration/photo by TO COME

Authors' acknowledgements
The authors would like to thank all the team at Macmillan Education in the UK and world-wide for everything they have done to help create *Inspiration*.

We are most grateful to Carl Robinson (Publisher, International Primary and Secondary) for initiating and overseeing the whole project so effectively and with such enthusiasm, Dulcie Booth (Senior Editor) for her energy, total commitment and attention to detail, Giles Davies (Design) for his creativity, and Sue Bale (Publishing Director) for all her support. We would also like to thank Julie Brett (Editorial Manager), Deirdre Gyenes (Managing Designer), Thomas Dartnall and Debi Hughes (Picture Research), and Caroline Boot (Teacher's Book) for their great contribution and professionalism. We are indebted to Anna Cole for her work on the Teacher's Book.

We would also like to thank James Richardson for his usual great skill in producing the recorded material and the actors who appear on the recordings and bring the book to life.

We owe an enormous debt of gratitude to teenage students and their teachers in many different countries who welcomed us into their classrooms and contributed so much to the formation of *Inspiration*. In particular we would like to thank teachers and classes in Argentina, Greece, Italy, Poland, Spain, Switzerland, Turkey and Uruguay. We are equally indebted to all those participants on teacher training courses in Europe, South America and elsewhere from whom we have learnt so much, in particular British Council courses in the UK and overseas, and courses at the University of Durham and NILE in Norwich.

Many individuals attended focus groups and commented on syllabus and materials, and we would like to express our great thanks to all of them, in particular Ursula Bader, Anna Bialas, Maria Birkenmajer, Sue F. Jones, Antonia Köppel, Malgorzata Lombarowicz, Urzula Nowak, Katarzyna Pietraga, Peach Richmond, Jean Rüdiger-Harper, Karl Russi, Ursula Schauer, Grzegorz Spiewak and Halina Zgutka.

The authors and publishers would also like to thank: Zoe Anastasis, Nick Barnes, Suzie Buckley, Ian Covington, Scott Fearn, Jane Hillier, Darren Hughes, David McMinn, Annabelle & Betty Mitchell, Rebecca Moseley, Imane Soussi, Ross Tudor, Reece Wilcox. Central TV Studios, Abingdon; Covent Garden Market; Department for Culture, Media and Sport; Four Spires Hotel, Oxford; London Transport Museum; London Underground Ltd; Profile Video; Riley's Pool Hall, Cowley; Startech.

We are grateful for permission to reprint the following copyright material: *Sitting On The Dock Of The Bay* Words and Music by Otis Redding and Steve Cropper copyright © East Memphis Music Corp, Cotillion Music Inc, Warner-Tamerlane Publishing Corp, Irving Music Inc, Rondor Music Limited and Warner/Chappell Music Limited, London, W6 8BS 1968 renewed 1975, reprinted by permission of International Music Publications Limited and Hal Leonard Corporation. All Rights Reserved. Adapted extract from 'Shakespeare's House' from *English Sketches* 2 (Intermediate) by Doug Case and Ken Wilson (Macmillan Publishers, 1995), reprinted by permission of Ken Wilson. *Do Wah Diddy Diddy* Words and Music by Jeff Barry and Ellie Greenwich copyright © Trio Music Co. Inc 1963, reprinted by permission of Carlin Music Corporation, London, NW1 8BD. All Rights Reserved. Culture Extract from 'Girls' by Stephanie Merritt copyright © The Observer 2001 first published in *The Observer* 18.03.01, reprinted by permission of the publisher. *Blowin In The Wind* Words and Music by Bob Dylan copyright © Special Rider Music/Sony/ATV Music Publishing Limited 1962, reprinted by permission of the publishers. All Rights Reserved. Extract on *I'm A Celebrity – Get Me Out Of Here*, reprinted by permission of ITV Press Office. *Girls Just Want To Have Fun* Words and Music by Robert Hazard copyright © Sony/ATV Music Publishing Limited 1979, reprinted by permission of the publishers. All Rights Reserved.

The authors and publishers would like to thank the following for permission to reproduce their photographic material: Aardman Animation pp92, 101(tr); ABPL pp60, 64 (chinese, burger, curry and spaghetti); Alamy pp19(9), 26(tl), 76(tr, tl), 86, 87, 88(br); BBC Research p50(Eastenders and Casualty); BBC Worldwide NHM p98; Brand x p64(pizza); Gill Brown p87; Alan Copson pp72(tl), 77(bl); Corbis pp16(tmr),21, 26(ml, b), 28(b), 29(mr), 30(bl), 33(t), 38, 38(t), 39(t), 40(r), 41(br), 62, 65(b), 74(b, c), 75, 77(br), 78, 88(tl, mr), 91(ml, bc, br), 95, 96(t), 104-5, 107, 117; James Davies p26(mr); Empics pp72/73, 77(mr); Mary Evans Picture Library pp32, 40(c), 43; Eyewire p52(whale); Freemantle p50(Neighbours); Getty Images pp26(tr), 27, 35, 42, 46(bl), 54, 66, 67, 69, 74(a, d, e), 91; Getty News and Sports pp16(tl), 72(tr); Ronald Grant Cinema Archive p38(t); Hulton p76; Hutchison pp30(bm, br), 73(b), 96(b); I'm A Celebrity Get Me Out Of Here / Granda Pic Desk pp80, 89(t); London Performing Arts Library pp56, 65(t); London Transport Museum p71(bl); Lonely Planet p26(tml); Kobal p39(b); Macmillan Education p33(phone, car, pen, camera, book, walkman); NHM p84(t, mr, br, bl); Photodisc p52(boy with surfboard); Redferns pp16(tml, tr), 28(t), 40(l); Rubberball Productions p52 (doctor); Science and Society Picture Library pp33 (film, rocket, helicopter), 71(br); S.M p19(6); SPL pp71(tr, tl), 84(ml), 88(t); Seven Network p50 (Home and Away); Yorkshire Television p51.

All commissioned photography by Haddon Davies p46, 53(c); Peter Lake pp6/7, 8, 9, 10, 11, 12/13, 14, 15, 17, 18, 19(4, 5,7, 8), 22, 24/25, 29(mr, br, bl), 34, 36, 41(models, locations and car), 44, 48, 49, 53(t, b), 57, 58, 68, 71, 77(tl), 82, 89(bl), 94, 96(b), 97, 100(tr), 101(tl, ml).

All other commissioned photographs by David Tolley.

Printed and bound in Spain by Edelvives
2009 2008
10 9 8 7 6